Theory As Prayer

Theory As Prayer

Beauty as a Measure of Human Dignity

Amardo Rodriguez

ISBN: 979-8-9886069-2-5 Paper
ISBN: 979-8-9886069-3-2 Hardcover
ISBN: 979-8-9886069-4-9 E/Book

Library of Congress Control Cataloguing-in-Publication Data is available upon request.

Public Square Press
102 Palmer Drive
Fayetteville, NY 13066
USA

For those who believe in the possibility of a better world.

Contents

Prologue

We all pray. What is different is how we pray, when we pray, whom we pray to, and what we pray for. But make no mistake, we all pray. We pray because we are of an infinite world that forces us to believe. We all believe something. We must. To believe is the essence of being human. What will become of us will be determined by what we believe and what we are vulnerable to believing. However, the world will often crush what we believe, reminding us how small and insignificant we are. It is in these moments, for sure, we will pray. We pray because we must believe.

So yes, I pray. I pray for all kinds of things, which means that I am always praying. But most often, I pray to understand. There are many things I want to understand. What I want most to understand are the limits of our potential. What are we fully capable of becoming? What are the practices, conditions, and arrangements necessary to become so? The writings in this book speak to these twin questions. I hope, even pray, that the insights I offer will be of value or of use to some.

We theorize because we are compelled to believe. A theory is nothing but an explanation. However, because we are bound by what we believe, there is no explanation of anything that will ever be final and perfect. But, for sure, some explanations will always be more valuable and useful than others. We would therefore be wise to always theorize from a place of humility. So, from what I am observing, based on where I am standing, this explanation seems to make sense. However, what I believe can change for multiple reasons, and what I am observing and understanding will change when this happens. We should take every theory with a grain of salt. There could always be a better theory coming around the corner. Our theories are human things rather than godly things.

We should also be mindful that theories can be circular, merely describing and affirming what we already observe and believe. Such, for instance, is the case with IQ. Defenders of IQ (who, by the way, refuse to go away) always forget to remind us that what passes for the study of intelligence must begin with somebody defining what intelligence is. What we are studying is what we subjectively define as intelligence or IQ. Regardless of how much we claim that our instruments are reliable and valid, there will never be an objective definition of intelligence. As for IQ having predictive value (which defenders of IQ cannot stop highlighting) if you control the design of something, you are also controlling many other things. In this case, in controlling what intelligence is, you control how intelligence is measured. So yes, intelligent people do better educationally, financially, and professionally. For argument purposes, let us take your word on this. But what was intelligent about more than 350 years of slavery, Black Codes and Jim Crow? What was intelligent about the Holocaust? What is intelligent about our destruction of the planet, our only habitat? What is intelligent about the creation and proliferation of weapons of mass destruction, which can now make for our demise with just one human error? Where are your prized and lauded high-IQ people in all this evil and madness?

Also, no law in the universe says that we should all value the same things, and that we are better off when we do. Thus, as much as we have the right to value the study of intelligence, other people should have the right to value the study of different things. In short, we should treat our theories as only our theories, explaining what we believe is important. We should always avoid imposing our theories on others. Let us all have our theories.

We also tend to theorize as gods — always trying to convince ourselves and others that our theories are perfectly capturing something going in a world that is outside and separate from us. I am in no way immune to this tendency. But I do my best to be mindful of it. I am in the small theory business. Yes, theory is important, but it can only take us so far. There is always a point when we must stop explaining and start doing. In the end, no amount of theory or theorizing can save us from doing all that is necessary to live justly, compassionately and generously.

I come to theory as prayer because I believe that we can make some sense of this world, and that doing so is important. I believe, however, that how we have been trying to make sense of this world is all wrong. For us, theory is an intellectual thing. Our goal is to create and generate as many theories as possible. We now have books full of theories for every discipline. However, I believe that theory is about attending to ourselves, trying to remove, to the best of our ability, all the things inside of us that limit what we can explain and understand. After all, theory is as much about what we are observing and describing as what we are explaining and experiencing. Therefore, before we can explain things more deeply and richly, we must be able to see things more deeply and richly. No amount of research techniques, instruments or protocols can help us do the latter. This kind of work involves attending to the things that shape our hearts. What shapes our hearts ultimately shapes our minds. Thus, theory is about finding the vulnerability to believe new things. It is about faith, as in praying for the strength to believe hard and difficult things. Pushing the limits of theory is about pushing the limits of what we are willing to believe.

Finally, prayer can be an offering, which means theory can also be an offering. Maybe what I understand can help you understand something better. Maybe it can help you resolve something. I therefore pray that my little theories can be helpful to you and enrich your life in one way or another.

One

Diversity and Faith

$\mathcal{N}$othing you are doing to promote diversity is meant to promote diversity. All that you are now doing is trying to protect yourself from diversity. That you are getting away with this delusion — that you are promoting diversity — is only because we are all, regardless of race and creed, afraid of diversity. We are afraid of what it demands of us. This is why the prophets must die. Change is hard. Change demands courage and fortitude, persistence and perseverance. Most of all, change demands faith.

We commonly say that faith is about believing in things unseen. But if that is true, then there is little to no difference between Hitler and Martin Luther King, Jr. How could this be right? How could these two people be morally and spiritually equal? I would say that faith is about how large a world you can imagine. How large a world you can imagine reflects how much faith you have. In other words, faith is about possibility, believing in a world where more things are possible. This is what distinguishes Hitler's faith from that of King's. King believed in a world where more things were possible. He believed that more things were possible through love. Whereas hate was at the center of Hitler's faith, love was at the center of King's. Faith is also about the things we use to imagine our worlds. What things you use will reveal what you believe is possible. Diversity requires a faith based in love. We must be willing to believe that more things will become possible out of the disruption that diversity will surely bring. Diversity will enrich us by enlarging us. This is the kind of faith that diversity needs to flourish. This is why nothing you are now doing will promote diversity.

For you, diversity can be neatly boxed, labeled, counted, and added. But diversity is ontological. It requires believing in a world where possibility is boundless. This is why you are hostile to diversity. This is why you always want to limit and contain it with all your rules, regulations and conventions. You have no intention of leaving it to its own devices. You believe that diversity and liberty are different things. This is why you never discuss diversity in terms of liberty. It is also why you have no qualms about suppressing liberty for diversity, or what you view as diversity.

For what is liberty? It is much more than the power to do things. It is ultimately about the power to believe things. We are shaped and defined by what we believe. If I surrender this power to you, then I have nothing. This is oppression. This is why all you are doing in the name of diversity is perverse and abominable. You are ultimately trying to control what we believe. We must believe as you believe. We must become like you or else face your wrath. In the name of diversity, we must homogenize and singularize. Your perversion and abomination are now our reality.

Two

MISERY AND SUFFERING

The problem with your life, or the reason for much of your misery, is that you believe you are important, and thus all you believe is no less so. However, there is nothing, absolutely nothing, in the universe that supports or affirms your assumption. This assumption is purely a creature of your own mind. Indeed, everything about the universe says differently. Nothing about you is important. From the perspective of the universe, you are nothing; absolutely nothing. In fact, this assumption of yours is much more than wrong. It is perverse. This perversion is the cause of your misery. It also makes you unpleasant to be around. Most of all, this perversion has made you a destructive person.

So, the next time you complain of someone offending and traumatizing you, remember that this experience is of your own making. It is only real to you because you believe that you are important. However, because what you are assuming is perverse, what you are now experiencing is such. This reality speaks to a key teaching in Buddhism: our suffering is always of our own making. In this case, you are making for your suffering by what you believe, which in turn is making for a view or perspective that is distorting and twisting your understanding of things. Our perspectives are all we have. However, as much as no perspective is perfect, when our perspective is engendering misery and suffering, then it needs examining. Something we believe or value needs to change. In fact, this is the work we should always be doing, examining everything we believe and value.

Three

PERSPECTIVES

Perspective is everything. It is also all that we have. Yet you insist on believing differently. You continue to believe, and would like us to also believe, that the way you perceive, experience and make sense of something is the only way to do so. Yet you claim to be this champion of diversity. But how can diversity flourish in a world that allows for only one perspective? Once again, we are reminded that our diversity is never the problem. It is you, always you. Your narcissism impedes diversity by your unwillingness to make space in your heart and mind for perspectives different from your own.

Four

Pandemics

We demand that everything be done to end this latest pandemic. We must do everything to stop this virus from spreading and creating variants. In our massive reaction to this virus and pandemic, we are assuming that humans are more important than viruses. No human should die from this virus. We supposedly have a right to stop this from happening. We therefore have the right to vanquish this virus from the earth. For us, doing so is morally acceptable. We are supposedly better off with this virus being gone.

But how did we come to assume that our life is more important and valuable than this virus or any virus? In fact, why our inability to even consider the possibility that the rise of this virus could ultimately prove to be good for us? Moreover, why do we assume that this virus's cost outweighs any future benefits? Where is the evidence that supports any of these assumptions? Indeed, why is there no consideration of the possibility that even though the rise of this virus could be deadly to some, it might be good for us as a species, and ultimately better for the planet? Again, such is the problem when we causally assume we are important. That is the problem when we fail to regularly challenge all that we believe. Our perspectives diminish. It never ends well.

Five

LEADERSHIP

*L*eadership is about difference. It has nothing to do with rank, position or even responsibility. It is about becoming larger and better versions of ourselves. As we become so, we become different and more amenable to who and what is different. Difference is born of strength. Strength means we can control our instincts and impulses. It also means we have the courage and fortitude to speak the truth as we see it and listen to it as others see it. We cannot make a difference in the lives of others if we cannot make a difference in our own. On the other hand, how much of a difference we can make in the lives of others will depend on how much of a difference we can make in ours.

Six

Racism vs Tribalism

I am now hearing that what we view as racism is really tribalism. Race is merely one way we do tribalism. As long as we remain tribal beings, we will devise ways to defend and justify our tribalism.

I am amenable to this emergent view because I never found race compelling in explaining over 350 years of slavery, Black Codes, and Jim Crow. Also, how does race help us explain Africans capturing and selling other Africans to Europeans? In using race as a framework, I am constantly reminded of what Audre Lorde said about how the master's tools will never dismantle the master's house. The oppressed are going to need a new set of tools to end oppression.

We have always said that race is an invention of racism — a concept brought into the world to justify one group brutalizing another. But race is an invention of our tribal instincts and impulses, the same ones that made it acceptable for Africans to enslave and brutalize other Africans. In this way, tribalism is a much more heuristic framework than racism. Of course, no framework can explain everything. But tribalism explains much more than racism. It also travels better. For if our goal is to understand how and why groups brutalize other groups, then tribalism travels better. Race has no purchase in many parts of the world. Further, tribalism has empirical support. We can now show that humans can use almost anything to establish in-groups and out-groups. We also know that these things can override race. There is nothing especially binding about race, gender, or anything else. Finally, tribalism gives us a much better understanding of what it will take for groups to stop brutalizing other groups.

For those who use racism as a framework to understand our history, the goal is to end racism. But ending racism does nothing to end tribalism. We can always devise something else to justify our brutalizing of others. In fact, racism saves us from looking deeply at our own tribalism. It gives us an out. Tribalism, on the other hand, pushes us to look much deeper. What, for instance, are all the ways we are tribal or hostile to other groups? Who is being victimized by all our various kinds of tribalism? How can we impede all our tribal instincts and impulses? So yes, ending racism is cool, but only by ending tribalism — or the most virulent kinds of tribalism, will we make it out alive.

Seven

LIBERALISM

*L*iberalism is about looking to government and the judiciary to secure certain various rights and liberties. Neoliberalism, on the other hand, focuses on shaping and controlling our social and cultural practices. Whereas liberalism is about changing laws and institutions, neoliberalism is about changing practices and arrangements. For instance, liberalism protects our free speech rights; neoliberalism contends that these rights, in allowing for hate speech, should be socially and culturally proscribed.

So, what does this all mean? Which movement should be encouraged? According to liberalism, anything that offends members of certain minority groups should be banned. Members of such groups supposedly deserve to be protected. But who exactly are these persons that need protection? Neoliberalism never tells us. In neoliberalism, groups are monoliths. One person can speak on behalf of all the members of any group. ("This is offensive to people of color") Indeed, neoliberalism is only concerned with group diversity. It has no interest in human diversity writ large. In fact, neoliberalism is hostile to such diversity. Such diversity belies its logic. For neoliberalism, diversity resides in groups. But such diversity is only partially true, abstractly true. There is also diversity in us, diversity between us, and diversity in the configuration of our different relationships.

Eight

LANGUAGE, LANGUAGE, LANGUAGE

You claim that I was "mansplaining." But another could claim that I was simply "dropping the knowledge." Even another could claim that I was merely explaining something important. And another could say that I was simply making a point that someone needed the courage to finally make.

But, of course, you would have us believe that only your description is correct. In your world, only what you feel and think matters. But why should we be complicit in propping up your delusion? What authority do you have to make such a determination, that only your description is correct? Why should we allow you to believe that you can remove diversity from human affairs? In fact, why should we even side with your view, that I am apparently mansplaining? After all, for all the different descriptions of what I did, yours reflects the least generosity. You would never want us to treat you this way. Indeed, you know nothing about me, just as I know nothing about you. But rather than beginning from a place of humility and generosity, you begin instead from a place of accusation and aggression. I am supposedly mansplaining. In doing so, I am a horrible person.

So, you end your note by saying that I should never again contact you to explain anything. There is nothing further that needs explaining. You have had enough of my mansplaining. Yet you remain convinced that you are a champion of diversity, say nothing about all your graduate degrees in communication. But how is that possible, you actually believing that you are a champion of diversity? How can diversity flourish in a world where people believe that there is only one truth? I would love to hear your answer to this question, but again, you demand that there be no further communication between us.

But this makes for my final point. Diversity makes communication possible. We suppress diversity by suppressing communication. That is, we suppress diversity by doing what you are now doing, believing that there is only one truth. This is why you end your note the way you do. For you, what is the purpose of any further communication when you already possess the truth? What is there for you to learn? But this is why vulnerability is integral to communication. Vulnerability means that I recognize that my view of something is merely that, my view of something. No truth is perfect and final. We are human beings rather than gods. Communication demands what diversity demands: humility, generosity and vulnerability. There will always be different descriptions, and our own could always be wrong.

Nine

OFFENSIVE LANGUAGE

*C*arl Sandburg College has a student code of conduct policy that states that any student who "is verbally abusive; threatens; uses offensive language; intimidates; engages in bullying, cyber bullying or hazing; [or] uses hate speech, disparaging comments, epithets or slurs which create a hostile environment" can face disciplinary proceedings from administrators.

The problem here is that there is no such thing as offensive language. It is purely a creature of language and culture, meaning only real to people of a certain language and culture. But why should the use of this kind of language concern us? Why should we oppose making university policy based on this language? One reason being that history teaches us a lot about the dangers of reifying things that are objectively false. There would be no slavery, no Black Codes, no Jim Crow, no Holocaust, without us believing false things. Believing things that are false stops us from acquiring the fortitude and resilience that come with dealing with things that are real. In other words, believing false things makes us susceptible to all kinds of neuroses and psychoses. On the other hand, our invention of things like offensive language, or our proclivity to believe in false things, reflects a lack of intellectual and emotional maturity. We invent false things to save ourselves from dealing with the rigors and demands of reality. In the end, however, we pay a steep price for believing in false things.

So, in this case, what is real? Human diversity is real. That language favors diversity is real. That life and the universe favor diversity is real. Indeed, human diversity is the constant. We will always be of different modalities, rationalities, sensibilities and spiritualities. We will always describe, perceive, experience and make sense of things differently. The purpose of "offensive language" is to tame and neutralize human diversity. Its goal is to singularize and homogenize. We must supposedly all agree that certain kinds of language are objectively offensive. Ultimately, our goal is to foster homogeneity, to use homogeneity to lessen human diversity. This is the insidious nature of using language like "offensive language" to make policy that is supposed to be about promoting diversity. The goal is to impede rather than promote diversity. Indeed, no diversity policy has anything to do with promoting diversity. The goal of any such policy is to protect the institution from diversity. For no institution can remain an institution without limiting and suppressing diversity.

Ten

TRUTH AND TRUTHS

*A*s always, Audre Lorde has a point, "we have no patterns for relating across our differences as equals. As a result, those differences have been misnamed and misused in the service of separation and confusion."

Diversity cannot flourish in a world where we believe truth is singular. This is the irony of all the diversity, inclusion, equity, and access commotion that is now upon us. We are approaching diversity from the belief that truth is singular. There is supposedly only one correct way to do diversity. Only one goal (inclusion) is permissible. There is, in fact, supposedly only one way to define diversity. In short, our own view of diversity will tolerate no diversity. Trifle with our model of diversity and we will cancel you. Because we believe that truth is singular, we believe that conformity is the path to diversity. We must therefore find offensive what you find to be offensive. Your enemies must be our enemies. We must make sense of things the way you make sense of things. This is the kind of homogeneity and conformity that diversity supposedly demands. Yet somehow, we continue to remain oblivious to our hypocrisy. How could conformity promote diversity? How could homogeneity be the goal of diversity?

But this is why we are now so excited about promoting, embracing and celebrating diversity. This diversity means nothing. It is diversity in name only. It threatens nothing. This plastic and cosmetic diversity is for you. It is you neutralizing a threat by coopting it. Now who could say that you are against diversity? Look at the elaborate diversity bureaucracy you have now created to include and promote diversity. Look at all the diversity training that is now mandatory. But again, all these things are for you. The problem with your model of diversity is that you believe that we can do diversity without doing diversity. We can therefore supposedly do human diversity without attending to the planet's biodiversity. The condition of one diversity has no relationship to the other.

Your view of diversity is shallow because your view of the human condition is shallow. Although we are racial beings, we are foremost ecological beings. The condition of our humanity is bound up with the condition of the world. The planet is becoming less and less diverse because we as a species are becoming less linguistically, ideologically, morally and epistemologically diverse. This is the case against colonialism and imperialism. In making human beings less diverse, both make the planet less diverse. However, with the rise and global proliferation of modern technology conquering time and space, the planet's diversity is now almost nothing. Never has the world seen this kind of conquest. On the other hand, never has the planet faced so much peril.

Saving ourselves, saving the planet, will require forging a new worldview that centers our ecological nature. What is best for us must involve asking what is best for the planet. If we were to apply this standard, we would quickly realize that all the diversity commotion that is now upon us is both dangerous and destructive. Ultimately, the goal is to singularize rather than pluralize. We want less diversity. Less diversity is supposedly best for all of us in the end. Diversity also supposedly needs hierarchy and bureaucracy to flourish. We believe that it must be surveilled and controlled for the good of all. What has emerged is a caricature of diversity — a diversity that merely looks like diversity. This diversity neither enriches nor enlarges anything. The loss of human diversity cannot be separated from the unsurpassed rise of human folly and stupidity. For what is bright and brilliant about destroying our only habitat, or the creation and proliferation of mass destruction where one person can now accidentally end the world?

Human beings were never meant to be in the singular truth business. History makes plain that this business never ends well. Diversity is always the constant. However, for us to come to terms with this reality, we will have to change how we view the world. This is what it will take to develop the patterns for relating across our differences as equals. We have to come to terms with our limits. We can only perceive, describe, experience and make sense of only so much. This is the kind of humility that diversity demands of us. In order to speak to someone who is different, and will always be different, I must believe that neither of us can command a perfect and final truth.

The fact that diversity is embedded within the world's order reminds us that communication is meant to be the order of things. We are supposed to listen to each other. Listening to each other allows us to learn from each other. When we are learning from each other we are also becoming less strange and estranged from each other. Communication is more than a linguistic and symbolic process we use to share things. It is about all the things we do to humanize each other and make ourselves less strange and estranged from each other.

Eleven

RHETORICAL BULLYING

There is a theory that claims that oppression begins in communication. Oppression represents the suppression of conflict, using communication to suppress conflict. Stanley Deetz (1992) has a taxonomy of the different ways we suppress conflict in communication:

I. *Disqualification* — can "occur through the denial of the right of expression, denying access to speaking forums, the assertion of the need for certain expertise in order to speak" (p. 187). For example, "You are White, what do you know about racism?"

II. *Naturalization* — "one view of the subject matter is frozen as the way the thing is. In this process, the constitution process is closed to inspection and discussion" (p. 190). In other words, treating something that is produced by human beings as natural and belonging to the world. For example, "How could you possibly say something so offensive?" In this case what is judged to be offensive is assumed to be made by nature rather than human beings.

III. *Neutralization* — "the values in the construction process are forgotten as arbitrary" (p. 191). There are always human values in communication. To make believe that any communication is devoid of

18

values is neutralization. For example, "That is such a vulgar thing to say. You should be ashamed of yourself." However, one person's vulgarity can be another person's honesty.

IV. *Topic Avoidance* — "every social group prohibits or discourages the discussion of some events and feelings." For example, "This conversation is making me really uncomfortable. Let us discuss something else."

V.   *Subjectification of Experience* — invoking one's opinion to stop any further discussion. For example, "This is simply how I feel, and I would appreciate if you would respect that and let us move on."

VI. *Plausible Deniability* — using ambiguity to conceal one's true position or opinion. For example, "I never said your presentation was horrible. I only said it needs a lot of work. No need to get hostile."

VII. *Legitimation* — rationalizing and justifying decisions and practices by invoking higher order explanatory devices. That is, using larger moral and ideological frameworks to justify various decisions and courses of action. For example, "Because I am a Christian, I simply cannot support your position on that matter." However, there is no one definition of anything, including what being a Christian means. Legitimation is about masking that fact.

VIII. Finally, *Pacification* — "the process by which conflictual discussion is diverted or subverted through an apparently reasonable attempt to engage in it" (p. 196). According to Deetz, "Messages that pacify tend to discount the significance of the issue, the solvability of the issue, or the ability of the participant to do anything about the issue" (pp. 196-197). For example, "Yes, I know this is an important issue and it matters a great deal to you. I get that and I really want to help you. But I doubt Congress is ready to take on such a divisive issue." But why must the matter be framed divisively, and who is assuming that the matter is inherently divisive?

If oppression begins in communication, by suppressing conflict, then liberation begins in communication, by emancipating conflict. Let all conflict bloom. I like this theory. It makes a valuable contribution to our understanding of oppression and reveals what liberation work looks like.

However, oppression also begins in the suppression of human diversity, in us rhetorically bullying others so that only one view, truth, or conclusion is upheld. We rhetorically bully and suppress diversity in the following ways:

I.   **The Illusion of Singularity** — assuming that language can convey and sustain a singular meaning. For example, "This statement is racist. It criminalizes and dehumanizes . . . immigrants while ignoring the hardships faced by them." Or "What you just said is really racist. You need to know that." But racist to whom exactly? Please, explain. How did you come to have this authority to objectively declare what is racist? Concepts like *Polysemy* (words have many meanings), *Polyphony* (different groups use the same language differently), *Homophony* (differently spelled words sounding alike), and *Heteroglossia* (using the same language to accomplish different goals and objectives) remind us that there is always ambiguity and confusion in language. There is always ***interpretive leakage*** and ***interpretive divergence***.

II. **The God Delusion** — assuming that human beings can command an objective view. For example, "How can you say something so offensive?" However, the fact that something is offensive to you does not mean that it is offensive to others. In fact, what one person views as offensive, another can view differently. No law in the universe mandates that how you view the world the rest of us should view the world. Our different experiences and circumstances make this kind of homogeneity and singularity impossible. Finally, when you say something is offensive, you are saying the entire world, like the remaining eight billion of us, should view the world the way you do. How did you come to believe that you are so special, that all of the world should view the way you do? Do you have any plans of viewing the world the many ways that

8 billion of us do? So why should we privilege what you feel over what we feel?

III. **Invoking Harm** — assuming that power resides in words and symbols. If words and symbols have power, then certain words and symbols have the power to hurt and diminish us. Case in point, for the sake of promoting diversity and inclusion, I now demand that you refrain from uttering certain words and expressing views that might cause "harm." That is, by invoking the notion of harm, I now gain the power to suppress any view I dislike, However, words and symbols have no inherent power to harm us. Harm comes from us having what analysts call an *external locus of control*—allowing our lives to be controlled by forces outside of us, such as the words of others. Hinduism, Buddhism, Stoicism, and many other traditions have long warned us about the dangers of being controlled by forces external or outside of us. We become strong, resilient, and independent by operating from an *internal locus of control.*

IV. **Denying Intent** — assuming that intent has nothing to do with anything. For example, "I have no regards for why you said what did. You still should never have said it." Or "There is no excuse for what you said. None." But who wants to live in a world where intent has nothing to do with anything? That is, who wants to live by this standard? To claim that intent means nothing is to claim that you possess a miraculous power to know exactly what is in another person's heart. Evidently, you are fully convinced that you are truly a special person. You possess extraordinary powers. You can somehow get language to do your bidding perfectly. But this is humanly impossible. Language will always be unruly. Without intent, communication becomes nothing. Thus, to take communication seriously requires us to take intent seriously.

V. **Invoking Morality** — assuming your morality is the only morality that should matter. For example, "Mary is so promiscuous." But why cannot Mary be described as generous? After all, sharing is caring. The reality is that no human being possesses the moral authority to objectively condemn what others are doing. This is the first teaching in moral philosophy. Your moral absolutism is a fiction and delusion.

VI.   **Language Creep** — using language to get around the fact that language is bound by meaning, and thus always subjective. For example, declaring that something is "clearly" racist, "obviously" racist, "plainly" racist, "patently" racist, "blatantly" homophobic, "outrageously" transphobic, and so forth. We are now to believe that language is no longer subjective and interpretive, and human diversity no longer matters. What the person said is "surely," "plainly," and "obviously" racist. But as Daniel Dennett of Tufts University reminds us, invoking the word "surely" is the most reliable sign of a weak argument. We can now add a few other words to this list.

VII.   **Invoking Rationality** — assuming there is only one way to make sense of something. "What you are saying makes no sense. No sense at all. What is wrong with you?" "People will laugh at you if they were to hear you saying such nonsense." However, that something makes no sense to you does not mean it makes no sense to others. In fact, why should something that makes sense to you make equal sense to the rest of us, like the other 8 billion humans on this planet? Where is this law written? Why do you believe that you are that special?

VIII. **Speaking for Others** — assuming you have the authority to speak on behalf of others. For example, "What you just said is offensive to Black people. You just need to know that." Or "Black folks are sick and tired of the President doing nothing about affirmative action." But when did all Black people gather in a certain place and give you the authority to speak on their behalf? When did this great gathering occur, and this authority given to you?

IX.   **Factualizing Facts** — assuming that your facts should be the only facts that matter. In other words, assuming that the facts that matter to you should equally matter to us. For example, "The fact is that Johnny took harder classes in college." "The fact is that Ken is overweight." In other cases, you say, "The reality is that John is wrong." But again, there is never one reality. Human diversity means that we are under no obligation to respect each other's facts. The facts you value can be different to the facts I value. I can recognize your facts without valuing them the way you do.

X.   **I and I** — assuming that others should be obligated to respect and even honor what you believe and value. For example, you believe that the Supreme Court is racist. It just "ended affirmative action." However, what about those Black persons who believe that rather than ending affirmation action, the Court rightfully "ended racial discrimination"? Why should we believe that only your description is valid? Indeed, nothing in the universe affirms the notion that we should care about what you believe and value. From the perspective of the universe, you are nothing, absolutely nothing.

XI.   **Labeling and Naming** — labeling and naming the person who is of a different view in derogatory ways so as to limit communication. In this case, refusing to allow a person to hold a different view. In holding a different view, the person nusr now be labeled and named something horrible. This strategy saves us from engaging the opposing view and confronting the fact that good people could hold opposing views for good reasons. This strategy thus stops us extending any empathy to those of opposing views.

XII. **Standardizing Standards** — assuming that your standards and measures are outside of time and space, ideology and politics, and thus universal. For example, "You sound like a damn fool when you say something like that." Yes, for some I may sound like a fool, but how do you know I sound like that to many others? What survey did you conduct? In short, your standards of anything are purely your own.

XIII. **No limits, no Humility** — assuming that there are no limits to what you can know and understand. That is, being oblivious to the fact that everything you know and understand is always bound to a perspective that, in turn, is shaped by your experiences and circumstances. For example, you speak in a binary way. When you speak, something is either right or wrong, true or false. For example, "What you are saying cannot be right?" But why must something be either right or wrong? Why can something not be something else?

XIV. **Invoking Emotion** — invoking your feelings to justify what is good, right, and just. For example, "I know that I was not the only person who felt uncomfortable when he said that word out loud." Or "I am really hurt by what you just said. Do you not care about what I feel?" That something makes you feel bad does not mean it was wrong for the person to say it. It merely means that it made you feel a certain way. You should also be reminded, as Buddhism teaches, that being governed by your feelings reflects weakness. For Plato, becoming learned begins in conquering ourselves.

XV. **Inventing Concepts** — inventing concepts that allow us to judge and condemn things we find abominable, like mansplaining, whitesplaining, and sexualizing. There are also concepts like "impermissibly uncivil" and "hostile climate." In reality, of course, these are purely subjective things, reminding us how language is always serving a political and ideological master. Let us also remember that racists and fascists invented concepts like "racial treason" and "race traitor" to condemn racial mixing.

XVI. **Inventing Threats** — claiming that in saying certain things, I am complicit in creating a context that poses a direct physical threat to members of a particular group. For example, "Universities are communities of staff and students first and foremost. They will always have a function of discussing difficult issues, but making minority members feel safe and welcomed must come first." Or "Saying what you just said puts our …… colleagues in danger." Or "Your comments are putting our …. students at risk of harm." Or "A student organization has invited a speaker to campus who has a history of inciting fear and distrust. While I am strongly in the support of first amendment rights, I am disappointed when those rights are used to make others feel unwelcome and even unsafe in our community." Or "We are well served by robust and ideologically diverse public discourse that includes radical, liberal, and conservative voices. But what you are saying is not that. You are being inflammatory." Really, says whom? I cannot now say anything that you subjectively judge to be posing a direct threat to anyone. No more am I simply being accused of being offensive. Now you are accusing me of making various people feel "unsafe" and "unwelcome." We are to forget that your description is subjective. Who is being "inflammatory" is subjective. But why must I be held responsible for the actions of others? Also, if I am now responsible for the actions of others, then are such persons responsible for nothing? In fact, how did I miraculously become responsible for the actions of others? Do you want to be held responsible for the actions of others?

XVII. **Asserting Truth** — using language to validate your truth. In this case, your truth is that what a certain person said is inherently and objectively racist. You want to convince us that this is not merely your subjective view. It is objectively so, as in "objectively offensive." It is supposedly a fact, outside of time and space. What the person said is "plainly racist," "overtly racist," "explicitly racist," or "flat out racist." However, such language cannot change the fact that your truth is subjective because you are a subjective being, purely a creature of a certain set of experiences and circumstances.

XVIII. **Ambitions & Ambitions** — invoking ambitions to suppress diversity. Fostering the impression that your goals are morally neutral, and thus supposedly serve no ideological interest. For example, language in a policy claiming that a university, in this case the University of Cambridge, seeks "to create a safe, welcoming and inclusive community which nurtures a culture of mutual respect and courtesy." "There is no place for any form of bullying, harassment, discrimination, sexual misconduct, or victimization in our community." But why mutual respect? According to Ross Anderson, "It is unreasonable to expect atheists to respect the views of religious believers, or to expect climate change activists to respect the work of earth scientists who are trying to make mining or oil drilling more efficient, or to expect campaigners for social justice to respect law professors who advise banks how to avoid regulation. What is reasonable is to expect members of the university to treat each other with tolerance and courtesy." But does the University of Cambridge treat every view with mutual respect? Is nothing ever judged abominable and intolerable? The fact is that noble ambitions, like maintaining civility, can insidiously function to suppress persons and positions we dislike.

XIX. **No Way Out** — framing the situation in a way that makes a different response morally repulsive. For example, "It feels wild to me that we're at this point in history and some folks are still not immediately signing a letter like this [calling for the canceling of a certain speaker that some judge abominable]. I'm sure you realize that not signing the letter is not a neutral stance." Or "Providing a veneer of respectability is part of what allows this group to do work that attacks the very lives of LGBTQ people in the U.S. & globally. Through your attendance you are personally complicit. . . in platforming and legitimizing this hate group." In short, you have framed the situation in such a way that I am now a horrible person for simply wanting to listen and form my own opinion. I must either fall in line or face your scorn.

XX. **Backdoor Language** — using supposedly neutral language that creates a backdoor for ideology, race, and culture. For instance, "I do not think it's helpful to characterize reasonable faculty concerns about exposure to a deadly pandemic as tyranny." Or "His tweets could be reasonably understood, and were in fact understood by many, to disparage any Black woman the president might nominate. As I wrote at the time, Mr. Shapiro's tweets are antithetical to the work that we do at Georgetown Law to build inclusion, belonging and respect for diversity. They have been harmful to many in the Georgetown Law community and beyond." But reasonable to whom exactly? What can seem reasonable to one person can be different to what it seems to another. This is human diversity. Also, how was the determination made that diversity is best achieved through inclusion, belonging, and respect? In fact, why should diversity be our aspirational goal? What is wrong with liberty, equality, and solidarity? Another example, "While we protect speech and expression, we work to promote civil and respectful discourse." Again, who is defining civil and respectful discourse, and why should our discourse be so? That is, which God opened the heavens and declared that our discourse should be civil and respectful? Another example, "I just want to assure all of you that The Post is committed to maintaining a respectful workplace for everyone. We do not tolerate demeaning language or actions. Editors [at *The Washington Post*] have made clear to the staff that the tweet was reprehensible and demeaning language or actions like that will not be tolerated." The problem here is that we are to assume that meaning is found in words and symbols. This is false. If meaning was found in words, then no one would ever say, "Yes, I know what I said, but that is not what I meant." Further, diversity means that two persons can have different interpretations of what constitutes reprehensible and demeaning language. The reality is that we will always describe and characterize the same things differently because of our experiences and backgrounds being different. To make believe that some things are devoid of ideology and politics, and thus obvious to all, is dangerous.

So why do we communicatively, discursively, culturally, and institutionally suppress diversity? We do so because we lack the capacity to deal with it. Diversity requires a tremendous amount of human development. It demands of us a dialogic and democratic temperament. We must be able to create time and space for truths and perspectives different from our own. Indeed, diversity is never the problem. It is us, always us. We never acquire the temperament to deal with the challenges it presents. Diversity is always the constant. As much as we try to suppress it, we will never successfully do so. This means that diversity, like conflict, will always come with anxiety. We will always be hostile to it, blaming it for one thing or another. However, if we are ready to put in the work, we can change our relationship to it.

Twelve

DOUBLE CONSCIOUSNESS

W.E.B. Dubois' notion of double consciousness means that Black folks are always viewing themselves from the perspective of White folks and measuring themselves by White folks' standards. One way we measure ourselves by the standards of White folks is through peer-review publishing, the kind of publishing we must do as academics to secure our jobs and advance our careers. Yet we do this kind of publishing knowing that no great intellectual work ever came from it. Toni Morrison, Ralph Ellison, Langston Hughes, Audre Lorde, James Baldwin, and company were all able to escape it. The rest of us, meaning those of us in academe, have been damaged by it.

Now we must take advantage of this diversity, inclusion, equity, and access moment by finding the courage to stop measuring ourselves by the standards set forth by White folks. This would mean telling White folks that diversity means that different people should be free to measure themselves by different standards of excellence. But we must be ready to fight for this freedom. Diversity demands struggle. For as Frederick Douglass once said, power surrenders nothing without a struggle.

Thirteen

God

God is in communication. This is why communication is hard. In fact, this is why communication is often impossible. It is also why communication demands so much from us, such as us recognizing that confusion is the nature of language, that context and meaning are bound up with each other, that meaning is in us rather than in words, and that empathy and generosity are vital for communication.

God is in communication because in achieving communication we become holy — less violent, less divisive, less destructive. In other words, achieving communication makes us democratic, pluralistic, and dialogic. We create space for the holy ghost, that which is beyond our imagination. So yes, communication is about words, meanings, and messages. It is also about medium and context. But communication is ultimately about expanding who and what we are ready and willing to understand. This is why God is in communication. We expand who and what we are ready and willing to understand by expanding our minds, hearts, and souls.

What communication demands of us is exactly what God demands of us. This is why God is in communication. We come to God in communication, in creating the vulnerability that understanding demands. Indeed, communication can never be about what is understood. After all, understanding is never final and perfect. Communication is also about what we are willing to understand. It is about pushing against the limits of what we are ready and willing to understand. This is a world of dark energy and dark matter. What we can know will never be any match for what we will never know. We limit God by limiting what we are ready and willing to understand.

Communication is about recognizing and removing all the things that limit what we can understand, meaning that communication is about removing all the things that limit our minds, hearts, and souls. In Buddhism, this is the quest for the empty mind, the mind that assumes nothing. A mind that assumes nothing expects nothing, desires nothing, fears nothing. In other words, an empty mind is an open mind.

This is why God is in communication. God demands of us an open mind, one that is vulnerable to everything. For instance, can human beings communicate with plants? Well, note how much we are assuming here. We are no doubt making many assumptions about communication. For instance, it is supposedly a linguistic and symbolic activity. However, how do we know whether our assumptions are valid? Why must communication be an inherently linguistic and symbolic process? This is how assumptions limit our minds, and ultimately limit what we are ready and willing to understand. God demands of us an empty mind. Emptying our minds is about making space for God. This is why God is in communication. How we do communication is about how we do God.

Fourteen

RIGHTS VS OBLIGATIONS

*I*f human beings have rights, as the US Constitution proclaims, where do such rights originate, from God or government? If our rights are from the government, then governments can also strip us of these rights. However, if our rights are from God, then no government has the moral authority to take them from us, and any attempt by the government to do so should be resisted.

However, the notion of rights assumes that human beings are individuals, outside and separate from each other. We are autonomous beings. But we now recognize that we are never outside and separate from each other. We are relationships. Whereas individuals have rights, relationships have obligations. We are obligated to help others become fully human. This means living in ways that create and provide all the resources others need to flourish. In helping others flourish, we flourish. From a relational perspective, our obligations to others are about our obligations to ourselves. In attending to others' prosperity, we are attending to our own.

To view ourselves as relationships rather than individuals would change everything. Our ethics and politics would be different. So also, our ideologies and epistemologies. But are we ready to view ourselves differently? Are we ready to treat others differently? Are we ready to demand much more of ourselves? This is the thing with viewing ourselves as individuals. It demands little from us. But look at the price we are paying for looking at ourselves this way? There would have been no slavery, no Jim Crow, no Holocaust, without individualism.

But now we need to go much further and view our relationality in terms of the world. Rather than merely relational beings, we are ecological beings. Our prosperity is bound up with the planet's prosperity. So rather than asking how we should live relationally, we now need to be asking how do we live ecologically? What kinds of minds do we need to be creating to live this way?

Fifteen

MONSTERS

Regardless of how hard you try to treat every person kindly, justly, and compassionately, you will always be a monster to someone. Every prophet was a monster to someone. The moral of the story is that you must always know your mind, heart, and soul. In this case, you must always know that you are a good person and that you will always do your best to treat others well. You must be strong enough to never let others turn you around and rob you of your joy. As much as others may try to demonize and monetarize you, you must always know who you are. We would therefore do well to always remember Audre Lord's words, "If I didn't define myself for myself, I would be crunched into other people's fantasies for me and eaten alive."

Sixteen

NECROPHILIA

*H*ow is it possible for supposedly educated people to still believe that meaning is found in words? I am referring to the legal philosophy known as Originalism — " the principle or belief that a text should be interpreted in a way consistent with how it would have been understood or was intended to be understood at the time it was written." This project is impossible as there is no way for us to ask a bunch of dead men from hundreds of years ago what they meant when they said certain things. Moreover, this project assumes that all these dead men shared a common set of meanings for certain things. But this too is impossible as all these dead men, even though racially homogenous, were of different experiences and circumstances. So what Jefferson meant by liberty could be vastly different to what Madison meant. Further, why should women and people of color be legally and morally ruled by a legal philosophy that is all about determining what a bunch of white men meant over two hundred years ago and desired for a country that is now racially, technologically, socially, morally, economically, and institutionally different in every way? Finally, why should we be willing to be ruled by people who are morally inferior to us, seen in the fact that these people held other people in servitude and bondage. What do we gain in remaining subservient to the will of these people?

We are interpretive beings. We interpret everything. Also, how we interpret things reflects our experiences, circumstances, and ambitions. Thus, nothing lends for one meaning. This can be seen in the Bible lending for endless denominations of Christianity. What then is behind the delusion that makes for Originalism? Why do so many judges, justices, and legal scholars believe that meaning is found in words? What is the value in doing so? But this is how delusions work. There is always something for us to gain. In this case, the delusion allows us to believe that we can be objective, in no way controlled by our passions and emotions, biases and prejudices. Also, in being objective, our experiences and circumstances have nothing to do with anything. For us, objectivity is good. We should value it and aspire to achieve it. Supposedly, being objective means that we are fair and impartial. We are, to use the words of Chief Justice John Roberts, merely calling balls and strikes.

But no judge or justice is merely calling balls and strikes. We are interpretive beings. Believing that we can be objective is about us wanting to suppress this fact. We will never rid ourselves of our biases and prejudices. In being interpretive beings, we are subjective beings. However, there is nothing inherently wrong with us being interpretive and subjective beings. We merely have to embrace it. There would be no human diversity without it. This is the problem with striving to become objective. We are to assume that human diversity is a problem. There must only be one measure, the one found in being objective. In representing that standard, one is supposedly representing the only standard that should matter. In this way, objectivity impedes human diversity by promoting conformity and homogeneity.

Originalism claims that the US Constitution lends for only one meaning, and this meaning is unalterable, cast in a historical moment. However, from an ecological perspective, things can only live and thrive by changing and evolving. In this regard, proponents of Originalism have a point in viewing a "Living Constitution" philosophy as a threat to Originalism. Originalism is about preserving and upholding that which is dead. It demands that the living look to the dead for moral and legal direction. We must remain oblivious to the fact that the dead, in this case, held other human beings in servitude and bondage. We must thus forget or be complicit in downplaying the fact that these people were evil.

The goal of Originalism is to protect the status quo, especially those who benefit the most in preserving the order of things. If sustaining a delusion is necessary to do so, then so be it. Ultimately, the goal of Originalism is to stop us as a society from changing and evolving. There must be no changing of what we believe and value. For those who profess to be religious, Originalism is the right way to approach the Constitution. But there is nothing godly in Originalism. Originalism is about worshipping the dead, and the Bible tells us that we should let the dead bury the dead. Life is for the living. Only those who are living can change and evolve. Rather than encouraging us to be biophilic, Originalism encourages us to be necrophilic. In this way, Originalism is an abomination. It would have the living be subservient to the dead. That life must change and evolve means that things must become different. Nothing that is living ever remains the same. In wanting us to look to the dead, Originalism wants us to defy the order of things. We must oppose change. Oppose diversity. Oppose life.

Seventeen

REVOLUTION

Revolution is about releasing ourselves of the practices, structures, and arrangements that others use to govern, pacify, and control us. It assumes that having no freedom to choose or create the forces and processes that shape our lives is debilitative and destructive. What emerges is alienation. In other words, the absence of freedom separates us from ourselves, and, in doing so, robs us of the capacity to act boldly and imaginatively. In this way, alienation robs us of our humanity. It makes us less human. We then act accordingly.

Revolution is about reclaiming control of our lives. It is about ending our alienation and dehumanization. I am nothing without the freedom to control the practices and processes that shape my life. I am reduced to a life that can never become extraordinary. I am damned to mediocrity. Thus, only through revolution is excellence possible. Only through revolution I can live with all the passion and imagination I can muster. Revolution is therefore much more about ending and dismantling things. It is about creating and inventing new things from places of liberty and freedom. In this way, revolution is about emancipating human diversity. It is about recognizing that the forces and practices that make your life valuable and meaningful can be different to mine. Our standards and definitions of excellence can also be different.

As such, revolution is about ending conformity and all the mediocrity that comes from conformity and homogeneity. Inclusion is oppression by a different name.

We choose revolution because time is finite. We also choose revolution because we have no control over when our lives will expire. Further, we choose revolution because there is no valid reason to simply surrender control of our lives to others, especially when our actions and decisions pose no threat to others. Personhood begins with consent. To suppress consent is to suppress control. On the other hand, reducing consent to autonomy is dangerous as no human being is really an autonomous being. In fact, autonomy is a delusion. We are relational beings, actually ecological beings. We become human through each other. Thus, consent, like control, will never be pure and pristine. It is instead simply about us doing our best to give each other the space to figure out our lives on our own terms. Finally, we choose revolution because we aspire to save ourselves and each other from the ravages of violence. When we believe that we have the right, for one reason or another, to impose our practices, structures, and arrangements on others, violence becomes normalized. Because the human experience is recursive by nature, meaning that as we do to others, so we become, violence begets violence. There will always be more and more violence we have to put up with. But herein resides the problem. The more we are shaped by violence, the more we are disfigured by it. As Frederick Douglass observed long ago, "No man can put a chain about the ankle of his fellow man without at last finding the other end fastened about his own neck." We choose revolution to save ourselves from the violence that will always fall back on us and diminish us.

Eighteen

AGAINST PERFECTION

We need to rid ourselves of the notion of perfection. It does nothing good for us. Even if we could have it, we should never want it. After all, what about perfection is valuable? After achieving it, what comes next? Where would meaning be found? What would be the reason to learn? In fact, what would there be for us to learn?

Language makes a lie of perfection. This is also how language saves us. It will never allow us to perfectly capture and share our thoughts and emotions. There will always be a struggle for language. But this struggle is necessary. This struggle for language is because we struggle to make sense of ourselves, make sense of each other, and make sense of the world. We struggle in all these ways because life is boundless. Nothing is ever final. Everything is always in flux. There is always possibility. However, most often we struggle badly by trying to make things lend for only one description and conclusion. Such struggles will never end well for us. Instead, we should embrace all the struggles that life presents. To do so is to remind ourselves that life is boundless. We will never subdue it. Our goal should be to explore it, engage it, and come to peace with it. We should therefore let go of the ambition to find complete and absolute truths. Instead, we should be about making valuable insights, those that expand our moral and epistemological imagination. For instance, discovering that language is inherently metaphorical is a valuable insight. It reveals that we can shape and change language in ways that make more things possible. We are in no way bound to war metaphors and viewing everything in terms of violent conflict.

We continue to believe that language allows us to distinguish those with superior minds from those with inferior minds. This is why all standardized tests (like SAT, LSAT, GRE) have a language component. Superior minds supposedly have a superior command of language. Even though this idea persists, we now know better. We now know that society makes mind and language. We also know that language makes mind, and different languages make mind in different ways. We also know that experiences make mind and language. We also know that relationships make mind and language. We also now know that we can reshape our minds by how we live. The moral of the story being is that mind and language are dynamic, elastic, and neuroplastic. Life has no interest in anything being one thing. All things are compelled to change and evolve. That our minds and languages are meant to change means that we are meant to change. We are supposed to perceive things differently, experience things differently, make sense of things differently. This, again, is why we struggle. I will never perfectly know how you understand something, just like how you will never know how I do. But this was never our problem. Instead, I just need to know that you are doing your best. This is why I am glad that language makes a lie of perfection. I would prefer us to be generous than perfect. That there is always more for us to understand means that there is always more for us to become.

Nineteen

FORM AND SPIRIT

There are many problems with identity. When you declare or announce that you are, say, a White, gay, man, you are saying nothing. For what being a White, gay, man means to one person can be quite different to what it means to another. Moreover, no person is merely a White, gay, man. This person can also be a brother, father, uncle, cousin, teacher, student, friend, neighbor, Christian, grandson, and choir member. Finally, identity is divisive. When you declare or announce that you are a White, gay, man, you are also declaring that you are *not* a Black, gay, man, nor a Black, gay, woman, nor an Asian, gay, man, nor an Asian, gay, woman, nor an Indigenous, gay, man, nor an Indigenous, gay, woman, and so and so on. How can you truly and genuinely identify with the issues impacting these people? That is, how is genuine solidarity possible when division and separation reign? Arguably, for such solidarity to be possible, we must be indivisible. We must transcend form (e.g., race, gender, sexual orientation, disability). We must recognize that form is a creature of thought, specifically a thought system that begins in division, separation, and fragmentation. Such a thought system will always create division, separation, and fragmentation. This is the problem with queer theory, feminist theory, and critical race theory. These enterprises are creatures of such a thought system, thus all obsessed with form and keeping us obsessed with form. For these enterprises, form is the new religion. There is also the policing of form. We must now speak in ways that form demands. Form is now God and master. However, as form rises, or the reifying of form deepens, let us note that the world is facing more and more peril.

There will always be form. An orange will always be different to an apple. The color of my skin will always be different to yours. The shape of my body will also be different to yours. Our problems begin when we reify form. We forget that form is a creature of thought, and thoughts are creatures of mind. Without mind, form is nothing. That form is now divisive is only because mind is divisive. Thus, for form to stop being divisive, our minds must stop being divisive, meaning that our minds must stop generating thoughts that make for division, separation, and fragmentation.

However, as much as there is always form, there is always spirit. We all share the same spirit. We all draw from the same well of life. Through spirit we are indivisible and inseparable. The problem with reifying form is that we forget we are spirit, and thus indivisible and inseparable. Attending to spirit heals our minds of division, separation, and fragmentation. Doing so also saves us from the delusions that division, separation, and fragmentation create. For instance, how could enterprises born in division, separation, and fragmentation, like queer theory, feminist theory, critical race theory, and even postcolonial theory, and that aim to keep us fixated on things that divide and separate us, possibly make for a world where division, separation, and fragmentation pose no threat to us?

We ultimately need a world where there is harmony between form and spirit. In such a world we would value both form and spirit. Thus, in such a world, we would never let race, gender, or anything else divide and separate us. After all, without spirit, form is nothing. However, achieving harmony between form and spirit will require a new mind. As Buddhism teaches, mind is everything. In order to stop bringing division, separation, and fragmentation into world, we have to stop creating minds that do so. This is our way out. We would therefore do well to heed to an old adage, "We cannot end a disease by spreading it."

This brings us back to identity. Identity distorts, diminishes, divides, separates. It does all of this by elevating form over spirit. Simply put, identity promotes egotism and narcissism. Identity is about who and what I am. However, no person is an individual. Human beings are relationships. We become human through each other. Identity has us focusing on the wrong things, asking the wrong questions. Rather than asking who you are, we should be asking what are you about? What kind of world are you fighting for? Identity politics stops us from owning our complicity in despoiling the planet, sponsoring the making of weapons of mass destruction, promoting mass incarceration, and doing many other ugly things. We are to blame only those with power and privilege for our oppression. But no amount of finger-pointing is going to save us. We all have blood on our hands. As Rabbi Abraham Joshua Heschel once said, "not all are guilty, but all are responsible." We would do well to focus on building new communities rather than obsessing with our identities.

Twenty

RIGHTEOUSNESS

Academe assumes that knowledge is everything. The more knowledge we can generate and disseminate, the better. Supposedly, knowledge makes everything better. However, rather than knowledge, the Bible says that we should hunger and thirst for righteousness.

Knowledge and righteousness are different things. One is about knowing what is right, the other about doing what is right. To hunger and thirst for righteousness is about forging the courage, resolve, and discipline to do what is right and just. It is about forming a certain kind of character.

Of course, many would contend that clearly and definitively knowing what is right and just can sometimes be difficult, even impossible. However, for the person who hungers and thirst for righteousness, what matters is the determination to do what is right and just. The absence of clarity has no bearing on resolve.

Academe assumes that by becoming more knowledgeable, we become better versions of ourselves. However, there is no evidence that affirms any correlation between knowledge and moral transformation. So, what then is the value of our obsession with knowledge? How do we continue to defend this enterprise that defines academe?

However, our problem is much larger than there being no correlation between knowledge and moral transformation. Our obsession with knowledge separates and detaches from the world and ourselves. Academe assumes that knowledge demands detachment. Objectivity is vital. We must strive to remove ourselves from the process. We must always be searching for the truth. Indeed, in academe, knowledge is truth by another name. To have knowledge, or at least any that matters, is to have truth. This is why we are to value knowledge. In generating and disseminating knowledge, we are really generating and disseminating truth. Thus, being obsessed with knowledge is about being obsessed with truth. But again, no amount of knowledge, and thus no amount of truth, translates to moral transformation. What then is the value of all this truth we are generating and disseminating?

Academe assumes that knowledge is outside of us. We supposedly acquire knowledge through discovery. This, again, is why we are to be objective, so that our knowledge is pure and pristine, free of human contamination. But no knowledge is ever so. We make knowledge just like how we make everything else. We make knowledge with our beliefs, values, and fears.

Being objective is about being dishonest and disingenuous. It is about upholding a lie. In this case, the lie being that the world is outside and separate from us. In reality, what we are finding in the world is what is in us. Our worlds are us, just like how our truths are us.

We fetishize knowledge in academe. We give it a power it will never possess. If our goal is to change the world, doing so will take much more than knowledge. It will demand nothing less than transforming ourselves. We can only do this by hungering and thirsting for righteousness, doing as the prophets command us to do. Only through righteous action will our redemption be possible.

Twenty One

PUBLIC SPEAKING

*I*f you want to understand colonialism or neocolonialism, just look at any communication curriculum in the United States. You will find that public speaking forms the foundation of every curriculum. Supposedly, public speaking is important. It makes for success and is vital to leadership. Supposedly, great leaders know how to use words to persuade and influence. At the core of public speaking is the notion that words have power, and thus commanding this power makes us powerful. We are to assume that this truth is applicable to all people, meaning that public speaking is good for all people.

However, in many places around the world, people believe that communication should be about listening rather than speaking. Listening builds character. It demands containing our egos. Through listening we discipline ourselves. We gain mastery of self. Thus, in many places around the world, communication is about refraining from speaking. It is about refusing to persuade and influence. As Sally Miller Gearhart reminds us, persuasion is violence. It is about violating the dignity of others by constantly having them view things as you do. Yet, how do you know that how you view things is correct? In this way, public speaking impedes humility. It also impedes reflection and contemplation.

The different perspectives reflect different worlds. In the world of public speaking, the focus is on individual success. We become successful through conquest, by being able to get others to do as we desire. Life is supposedly a struggle. We are either winners or losers. What is right is what allows us to win. This is why public speaking matters. However, what now to make of the fact, as seen in the notion of confirmation bias, that no one has the power to persuade us of anything, regardless how eloquent the person, or how compelling are the facts. In the end, we will believe what we need to believe.

Public speaking is a performance. It is about making believe that we have power. With our words we can bend reality to our will. We can be gods. But confirmation bias makes a lie of the claim that our words have power, and ultimately a lie of the other claim that public speaking gives us power. Simply put, confirmation bias cuts us down. It returns us to our humanness. We will never be gods. Yet this is probably the problem all along, our unwillingness to come to peace with our smallness and humanness.

From the perspective of the universe, we are nothing. Yet our blessedness resides in our nothingness. Rather than focusing and obsessing with ourselves, we can now appreciate and be in awe of how grand and magnificent the universe is. If we were to gather up all the pebbles on all the beaches in the world, our planet would be merely one pebble. We are, again, nothing. Yet we insist on believing that we are important and have the power to do important things. But the ecological peril that is now upon us makes plain that us believing that we are important has done nothing good for us. It has only made for misery and destruction. Our redemption resides in us embracing our nothingness. This involves dismantling all the moral, ideological, and epistemological practices and arrangements that would make us believe that we are important and have the power to do important things.

Twenty Two

WORDS, WORDS

I now understand why we are unwilling to let go of the notion that words have power. If words have power, then commanding words, we have power. However, if words have no power, then we have no power. But what of all the incoherence? For instance, as much as we claim that words have power, we also claim that actions speak louder than words. In fact, we also say that without actions, words mean nothing. Thus, what gives? Do we want actions or words? After all, if words have power, why must we bother with actions? On the other hand, how can we complain about hateful and harmful words impacting us when such words are never associated with hateful and harmful actions or intentions?

Also, we claim that words have power, but would never admit that words have power on us. For instance, the same person who says that words have power would never claim to hate, say, Black people because they listened to speeches by racists. However, if words have power, why do the words of racists have no impact on those people?

There is another kind of incoherence. To believe that words have power is to believe that others can hurt us with words. However, what becomes of agency and strength if others can hurt us by merely using words? How can I claim to be strong if you have the power to hurt and harm me with your words? Evidently, if words have power, then I have nothing. But again, who admits to having nothing, as in having no agency?

Our way out of all this incoherence is to finally admit that words have no power. But this would mean taking responsibility for our lives. Nothing ever needs to be about us. If something is about us, it is because we have chosen to make it so. In this case, no law in the universe says that I should allow your words to hurt and diminish me. That is a choice, and just as much as I can make one kind of choice, I can also make another kind of choice. Indeed, without agency I can only be a victim. So, by embracing agency, I am choosing to be a champion rather than a victim.

Twenty Three

LOCATING GOD

For many of us, God is an entity that is outside and separate from us. We bow and kneel before this God. But, of course, this God is purely a creature of our imagination. However, is this God, which is outside and separate from us, working for us? That is, is this God saving us from violence? In fact, why must we limit how we can imagine God? Where is it written that God demands this of us? Indeed, what do we gain in limiting what God can be and ultimately what we can be?

Twenty Four

POWER

*H*istory teaches us a few important things about power. First, people who desire power will find any excuse or circumstance to acquire more of it. Second, people who acquire power rarely return it without a struggle. Finally, people who desire power always want more of it. No amount is ever enough.

We should never encourage these tendencies and proclivities. The reason being that power is an abomination. It is about us wanting the means to do things that we have no business doing, which is seeking to control the lives of others. In short, power is about robbing others of control of their lives. In this way, power dehumanizes. For without the means to shape our lives, we become separated and estranged from ourselves. We lose the ability to act boldly and creatively. Alienation becomes our reality, as well as all the neuroses and psychoses that come with being so. Thus, power dehumanizes us by suppressing the fact that the condition of our lives is our responsibility.

We need autonomy to decide what is best for us. That we are responsible for the condition of our lives means that we must always carefully examine the consequences of our actions and decisions. This is how we recognize that we are ecological beings. Our actions always have consequences, just as much as the actions of others. What is best for us must now be seen ecologically rather than individually. In this way, power dehumanizes us by blocking our moral evolution. It stops us from recognizing how my humanity is bound up with yours. Thus, there is always selfishness and peril in a world that encourages us to acquire more power. Worse, there is always a perverse sense of what it means to be human. So, it is not merely the fact that power corrupts, but it disfigures, diminishes, and, ultimately, threatens.

We hear in song that rulers make for bad lovers. This is no doubt true. The reason being that power impedes empathy and compassion, tenderness and selflessness. It makes us hard and rigid, belligerent and intolerant. Power is about lacking strength, such as the strength that is necessary to leave people alone. In other words, power is weakness. Thus, power is always about control. But this control is never perfectly attainable. So power is always about acquiring more power. No amount of power is ever enough. There is always a case for more rules, more laws, more regulations. Power means conformity. Power means assimilation. In other words, power means the smashing and vanquishing of diversity. This is why power is an abomination. Diversity is the order of life. We will always be different in one way or another. This, of course, is not to say that our differences are morally equal. Instead, it is merely to say that our differences must be navigated and negotiated.

Diversity makes communication possible and necessary. Yet, this is also how power vanquishes diversity. It does so by depriving diversity of communication through laws, rules, and regulations. No opposing view will be heard, or at least taken seriously. Diversity becomes background noise. In this way, power reduces communication to nothing. But in reducing communication to nothing, power reduces us to nothing. For what is communication? It is constitutive. Through communication we form ourselves, our relationships, our worlds. However, how we do all these things will depend on how imaginatively and courageously we can do so. In other words, communication is about how we form and transform our being. To rob us of communication, the ability to interpret the world richly, is to rob us of our humanity.

Power comes in different ways. There is, of course, the power that comes with acquiring the means to make and impose laws, rules, and regulations. There is also the power that comes with being able to create structures and arrangements that can do your bidding. Then there is the power that comes with being able to shape my mind like yours, and thus have me make sense of things the way you do. However, there is also the power that comes with being able to deprive me of the resource I need to view the world differently. In other words, power is about all the insidious ways we suppress diversity, such as seeking to convince me that my diversity is abnormal, immoral, and pathological. In this way, power is about convincing me to destroy my own diversity.

Power and violence cocreate each other. Power cultivates violence, and violence realizes power. There can be no getting rid of one without the other. If we wish to rid the world of violence, we must rid the world of power. This is the challenge we now face. As we have become increasingly destructive, the world has become less and less diverse, and more perilous. Actions have consequences. We save ourselves by impeding our own proclivity to control others.

Twenty Five

OPPRESSION

Oppression is about who gets whom to believe, value, and desire what. That is, if you can have me believe what you believe, and doing so serves your interest, then that is oppression. Conversely, liberation is about being able to believe differently. So, if you believe that human inequality is real, then I should be able to believe differently. If you believe that hierarchy is natural and necessary, then I should be able to believe differently. If you believe that violence is necessary, then I should be believed differently. If you can stop me from believing differently, that is also oppression. I am by no means naively suggesting that oppression is purely a discursive affair, but merely to remind us that what we believe matters, and thus who controls what we believe is important, very important.

I am believing differently is about our aspirations being different. The world you want is different to what I want. I believing differently is also about our ancestors being different. What I owe my ancestors is different to what you owe yours. Also, I believing differently is about I being of a different imagination. Our beliefs shape the limits of our imagination. Thus, for us to imagine the world differently, we must be willing to believe differently. So, for all these reasons, I choose to believe differently.

This is how I look at the struggle between oppression and liberation. Who is successfully imposing their beliefs on others? Who is stopping others from believing differently? On the other hand, how are these efforts being resisted and contested? What new beliefs are being advanced, and what do these beliefs promise?

As much as I like what I believe, I never want to impose what I believe on others. I am about making space for all of us to believe differently. If human diversity should mean anything, it should mean us being able to believe differently, as long as doing so poses no direct threat to others. For as much as I like what I believe, and I am confident you also like what you believe. So let us come to an understanding that promotes peace.

What we believe shapes everything. This is why I look at oppression and liberation in terms of what we believe. You have complete control of my mind, body, and soul when you can get me to believe what you believe. Never again can I be a threat to you. In controlling what I believe, you are, besides controlling what I value, ultimately controlling what I can imagine. This, as many now say, is simply a bridge too far. Why should I allow you to have all this control over me, especially when I have no ambition to have such control over you? What do I gain from this? In fact, what does the world gain in all of us believing the same things, and only those things set forth by you?

Twenty Six

ACADEMIC EXCELLENCE AS IDEOLOGY

This you are never told when you are training to become an academic. To be a successful academic, you must meet certain expectations that are simply assumed to represent a model of excellence that has nothing to do with ideology, and thus serves no racial, cultural, or political interests. It is pure and pristine, outside of time and space, given to us by gods rather than mortals. This model of scholarly or academic excellence demands of us the following:

- Peer-review publishing. We must always be publishing, but only peer-review publishing matters. So even though no important idea is yet to come out of the peer-review process relative to the many that have come out from other processes, along with the fact that we have long known that the process is arbitrary, peer-review is still the standard we must uphold.
- Journal Rankings. We must not merely be always peer-review publishing but publishing in only top-tier rather than second or third-tier journals. In short, we must uphold the distinctions among scholarly journals.

- Indexing. How much our work is being cited and referenced matters. Even though you are being cited and referenced means nothing, especially since you will be doing most of the citing and referencing of your own work, prepared to always know your index citation number.
- Authorship position. Authorship position matters when you are peer-review publishing in top-tier journals. Ideally, you need to be first author, the one with the corresponding information on the article. You also need your papers to be endlessly cited and referenced so you can have a high Google Index score. You can help with this by citing your own papers again and again and encouraging your students and advisees to do likewise.
- Awards. Your peer-review papers and books need to win awards. This is all that matters for your work to be judged as excellent. There is no need to demonstrate that your work actually changed anything or made anything better.
- Lead Articles. Your articles need to be the lead articles in journals. Where your publication appears matters, even if this is purely determined by the whims of the editor and history makes no case of this being important or relevant to anything.
- Quantity of publications. You must always be publishing and publishing and publishing. Quantity is everything.
- Publishers and publishers. The distinctions found among journals are also found among book publishers. University presses are valued over other scholarly presses. In fact, among university presses, ivy league presses are valued over other university presses. Whether your Harvard University Press book will change anything has nothing to do with anything. What matters is how your book came into the world rather than its promise to change the world.
- Individual awards. You need to get awards from various national, international, and regional declaring you are a distinguished scholar. Never mind that you are being nominated by your friends, girlfriends, boyfriends, and lovers who you will then nominate for other awards in the future.

- Editorial boards. You need to be on editorial boards. But again, because of the distinctions among journals, you need to be on the editorial boards of the most prestigious journals.
- Named professorships. You want to be more than merely productive enough to be a full rather than assistant or associate professor at a top-tier or "Research One" university. You want ultimately to be a named professor.
- Emeritus. Even in retirement, you still have a last measure to meet. Your body of work must be examined by your department and college colleagues to determine whether you deserve the title of emeritus, and all (and only) the library and parking privileges that come with it.

Academe has all manner of devices and processes to bind us to this ideology of academic excellence. The consequences that come with refusing or failing to conform and submit can be severe, such as never getting an academic appointment where you have the time and resources to do the work you want to do, or receiving tenure and promotion, or establishing job security, or getting decent merit raises, or getting library privileges upon retirement.

There is always ideology and will always be ideology — a system of beliefs, values and desires that a certain group uses to determine what is real and important. We are merely to remember that ideology performs a set of key functions:

I. Encouraging us to forget that we are dealing with things made by mortals rather than gods.
II. Encouraging us to forget that what passes as real is nothing but a creation of a certain belief system.
III. Encouraging us to forget that what passes for real is always serving a certain interest and impeding other interests.
IV. Encouraging us to forget that what is real is always sustained by a variety of structures and arrangements.
V. Encouraging us to forget that what appears to be real is self-reinforcing and self-perpetuating.

VI.   Encouraging us to forget our own complicity in sustaining what is real, and thus how we are seduced only because we are vulnerable to being seduced.

VII. Encouraging us to forget that what is real can be fundamentally different to what is important. In other words, ideology is always seeking to convince us that what is real is important, even necessary.

Evidently, undermining a dominant ideology is no easy thing. Besides shaping for us what is real, ideology also shapes how we live and embody what is real. What then does revolution demand of us?

In this case, how do we get out from under the dominant ideology in academe? As of now, we believe that the struggle should be about adding more color and flavor — appointing Blacker and Brown editors, hiring more Black and Brown faculty, putting more Black and Brown people on editorial boards, publishing more Black and Brown scholars. But all these initiatives, though helpful for many Black, Brown, and Indigenous people, pose no threat to the dominant ideology in academe. This is a case of mistaking inclusion for revolution. History teaches us again and again that revolution demands sacrifice. This is where Hinduism and Buddhism can help us. What we must be willing to sacrifice is our ego. We must be ready to do our work for purely the sake of doing it. We should expect no reward. This is the practice of detachment, never allowing our desires to control us. We must be our revolution. If our scholarship is to be different, and thus the reasons for doing it to be different, we must be different. No ideology simply takes hold of us. There is always complicity, consent, and agreement. Detachment is about ending all of this. It is about recognizing that a better world can only come from a better us.

Twenty Seven

THE WAGES OF VENGEANCE

There is nothing more corrosive and destructive than vengeance. It destroys mind, body, and soul. This is why nearly every prophet warns us about it. Vengeance makes us evil, ultimately making the world evil. In other words, through vengeance we bring evil into the world by becoming evil.

Neuroplasticity says that we shape our minds by how we live. Vengeance makes this plain. When we are vengeful, we diminish our minds. Thus, if our goal is to expand and enrich our minds, we must refrain from vengeance. In fact, if our goal is to heal our minds and ultimately heal the world, we must stay away from vengeance.

What are we now to make of medical students in psychiatry departments at prominent US colleges demanding that professors be fired for saying anything that some find offensive? How could these students, who on paper are supposed to be studying the wellbeing of the mind, know nothing of the corrosive and recursive nature of violence? What do such incidents reveal about the current state of psychiatry? Would these same students, upon graduation, counsel their patients to be vengeful? Do they genuinely believe that vengeance has a place in the healing of the mind? Thus, why do they now believe that nothing less than the firing of a professor is necessary, even after the professor has profusely and publicly apologized to right a wrong?

There is for sure much evil in the world. However, we should never forget all of it is our making. We bring evil into the world by being evil. Also, because of the recursive nature of the human experience, when we do evil, we become evil. If there is any possibility of a better world, we must refrain from vengeance. But we must ultimately do more than simply refrain from doing evil. We must do what is beautiful. The world can only become beautiful when we become so. We must therefore be ready to forgive, and forgive again and again, just like how the prophets advised us to do. Forgiveness heals us, and in doing so is integral to the healing of the world.

Twenty Eight

THE PROBLEM WITH RACISM

When I accuse you of racism, I am charging you with blocking my progress and success. Charges of racism say that I want this to end. I want all of the impediments to be removed. I want to get what is mine, what I deserve. This is the problem with race politics. It has nothing to do with changing or improving the world. It is instead about making the world better for the advancement of my race, or those are presumably of my kind. In this case, stopping others from treating those of my race poorly and prejudicially. This is why identity is important when race matters. But what of all the world's other peoples? In fact, what of the world's other living beings? Who is going to care for these other peoples and beings? Why should we only care for those who racially look like us?

Race would make us believe we are separate from other peoples and species. But this is also what makes race a dangerous notion. In reality, there is no separation or division between us. We are all, first and foremost, organic beings, bound by the same ecological rules and rhythms. Our prosperity is bound up with each other. We must therefore be always looking out for each other. We only do well when all living beings are doing well.

Twenty Nine

COMMUNICATION

Communication is constitutive because it is discursive, recursive, and performative. This is what makes the study of communication important. It creates the center. It sustains the center. We must make sense of things together, always together. The negation of communication is not confusion. It is isolation. Isolation obliterates us.

Communication is constitutive because all that human beings will ever have is a perspective, and our perspectives will always be different because of our different experiences and circumstances. Communication is what allows us to explore, navigate, and harmonize our different perspectives. In short, communication assumes diversity. There will always be perspectives that are different to our own. Diversity succeeds only when communication succeeds. Conversely, when communication is suppressed, diversity is suppressed. If you therefore want a world that values diversity, then work for one that values communication.

Thirty

SEARCHING FOR DIFFERENCE

We all believe we know what love is. We have felt it, been through it. We have also struggled with it, been wounded by it. So, of course, we know what love is. Who is so dumb to even ask? But what we commonly define as love is nothing but infatuation. It is a feeling. It demands nothing much from us in terms of integrity and character. Supposedly, the heart wants what it wants. We claim that we cannot help who we fall in love with. Our minds supposedly have nothing to do with love. We claim that "Love makes us do foolish things." It is also a mystery. We supposedly have no control over it. Just as mysteriously we can fall into it, just as mysteriously we can fall out of it. We are therefore never to say "never" when it comes to love.

What we do with love we also do with difference. We are convinced that we know what it is. Difference is supposedly found in us being of different things, like different races, genders, and so forth. We can see it. Whereas we know love by feeling it, we know difference by seeing it. We also believe that difference demands tolerance. We must tolerate each other's differences for the common good. We should also include difference. Inclusion is supposedly best for difference. It is also presumably what difference wants. But like with love, what we believe about difference is all silly.

Difference has nothing to do with things like race, gender, and sexual orientation. Viewing difference in terms of these things is like calling an ocean a body
of water. In a sense such a description is true, but in a much larger sense such a
description is absurd. Also, inclusion does nothing good for difference. Inclusion is assimilation by another name. How can difference remain difference
after it has been neutralized, pasteurized, and deodorized?

What love demands of us is no different to what difference demands of us.
Love demands generosity of mind, body, and spirit. In a word, love demands
selflessness. As found in the words of a song, true love asks for nothing. Love
also demands empathy and compassion, kindness and tenderness. Moreover,
love demands courage and fortitude, resilience and perseverance. In short,
love is an expression of mental, emotional, and spiritual strength. We must be
strong to love. Difference is no different.

We have to be strong to deal with difference, to resist our impulse to assimi-
late and neutralize difference for our own convenience. Difference is also
about that which is different to what we believe, value, and perceive as real.
It assumes that different things can be true without other things being false.
Also, difference assumes that no truth is ever complete and absolute. Truths
can change, evolve, and mature. Finally, difference assumes that no human
being can command a perfect or final view or understanding of anything. All
human beings have limits, and these limits shape and guide our truths. Thus,
for difference to flourish, we must resist our impulse to judge and condemn.
This involves strength. Also, for difference to flourish, we must resist our
impulse to believe that the world revolves around us and therefore we should
be the final arbiters of all things. Finally, for difference to flourish, we must
resist our impulse to singularize and homogenize. This too requires strength.
Thus, for difference to flourish, like love to flourish, we must be able to do
many hard and difficult things, meaning that we must be mentally, emotionally, and spiritually strong. Difference is therefore not found in things outside
and separate from us. Instead, difference is found in us. It is about whether we
have the strength to refrain from hate, vengeance, and violence. It is also about

vulnerability, as in our willingness to perceive, experience, and make sense of things in new ways.

However, when we are weak, we assume that difference is found in things outside and separate from us. We therefore believe that in attending to things like race, we are attending to difference. In fact, we believe that in advancing things like race, such as fighting for the inclusion of race, we are advancing difference. Ultimately, what emerges is an obsession with these things. Every vast and ever-expanding diversity bureaucracy reflects this. However, there is no difference in things like race. We are merely to assume that because our races are different, we are different. But, of course, this is false. We can be of different races and share a common worldview. On the other hand, we could share the same race, yet be ideologically, religiously, and epistemologically different. Further, the differences that matter to one person can be different to the differences that matter to another. So, whereas you view a person's race diversity as being important, another can view the person's ideological diversity as being so. Finally, how one person experiences being of a certain race can be different to another of the same race. That is, two Black persons can have different views of what it means to be Black. What then becomes the value of viewing both persons similarly, as in assuming that sharing a race makes for a common denominator? Indeed, rather than promoting difference, race diminishes all the diversity within us and between us by artificially and superficially reducing our diversity to a few arbitrary and abstract things. Again, the fact that a person is racially different in no way means that the person is morally, ideologically, or epistemologically different. What then is the difference that the person represents by merely being of a different race? What difference are we supposedly adding or achieving by including a person of merely a different race? Also, why should this racial diversity have more purchase than, say, epistemological diversity?

To reduce difference to things like race is to reduce it to an abstraction. When it becomes so, it becomes nothing. Thus, for all our talk about valuing difference, we want nothing to do with it. Our goal is to diminish and destroy difference. We seek to do so because we are weak. We lack the strength to create difference. So rather than finding it inside of us, we believe it is in things outside of us. We choose to forget that those things are made by us, reflecting all the things we believe, value, and desire. But delusions always make for perversions. So, in our goal to promote diversity, we are really promoting conformity. We must all now find offensive what you find to be so. We must all be outraged at the things that outrage you. We must all condemn who and what you condemn. We must all arrive at the same conclusion as you do. We must all interpret things the way you do. We must all agree with your approach to resolving a matter, such as terminating the person who used a racial slur. If we are ever to do differently, then we must be ready to face your wrath. Thus, because of your weakness, we have come to believe that violence is vital for the flourishing of difference. Those who offend us must be subject to pain and misery. We are therefore to foolishly believe that the same things that make for evil, like hate, vengeance, and violence, can make for good.

We must do much more than recognize that difference, like love, begins inside of us. We must also recognize that difference and love are bound up with each other. We create and generate difference by creating and generating love. This is the lesson found in the life and teachings of Jesus Christ. Love transforms us. It gives us the strength that difference demands of us. In doing so, love gives us the tenderness and kindness, empathy and compassion, grace and generosity, that difference demands of us. Thus, what now passes for a problem supposedly born of difference, such as a person saying something that many find to be racially offensive, really has nothing to do with difference. It is instead about our failure to create and generate the love that difference needs to flourish. We therefore need to stop blaming our diversity problems on our differences and calling for us to get pass our differences. Our problems never had anything to do with our supposed differences. Instead, our problems originate in our weakness, our inability to forge the mental, emotional, and spiritual strength necessary to save ourselves from hate, vengeance, and violence. Without love, difference is impossible.

Thirty One

LOCATING DIFFERENCE

Once again, we must return to Audre Lorde's notion about how the tools that build the house of the master will never build the house of the slave. In this case, if those who enslaved and brutalized other human beings believed that difference is found in things like race, how could those who now claim to be on the other side of history view difference as being in the same place? What then becomes the possibility of liberation when both oppressor and oppressed view the world similarly? But this is where we are in the current age of diversity, equity, inclusion, and access (DEIA). We are here because this movement threatens nothing. That is, we are here because this movement poses no threat to us. This is why both oppressor and oppressed like the idea of difference being in things like race rather than in us. It allows us to manage it as something that is in things. In this case, we can manage difference through rules and regulations, procedures and processes, structures and arrangements. If there is ever a supposed diversity problem, all we need is another regulation or position to fix it. We believe that with enough regulations and positions, difference will be fine.

But such will never be the case. Every new regulation and position seek to promote conformity rather than diversity. However, this puts us in conflict with the world. Life moves towards diversity, flourishes in diversity. As such, every new regulation or position, in threatening diversity, threatens life. Such are the wages of promoting conformity. But life will eventually push back. Regardless of how determined we are to vanquish difference, we will never succeed in doing so.

The life of Jesus Christ is about difference. For the authorities, Jesus Christ was a threat. He was different. He believed and valued different things. For those with power, such difference was a problem. It was too much to be tolerated. It had to be vanquished. Violence was necessary. In other words, if the status quo is to be preserved, violence is necessary. Only so much difference can be tolerated. Supposedly, to allow difference to rise above a certain threshold would be to ferment chaos and threaten the status quo. So again, to preserve the status quo, difference must be sacrificed. Such is the peril of difference. It is always facing the threat of violence. What then is difference now to do? How could difference also resort to violence and still be difference? Thus, difference must do differently? Instead of violence, difference must choose love. This is how we know difference. It chooses love.

This is the problem with the DEIA movement that is now upon us. It promotes violence rather than love. We are now to believe that we can achieve diversity by constructing a vast diversity bureaucracy. However, the goal of any bureaucracy is to vanquish difference. It does so by convincing us that difference is a threat, which involves constructing and manufacturing difference as threat. Because difference is supposedly so, it is deserving of either regulation, investigation, or termination. A vast bureaucracy is necessary to perform all these functions. In short, a bureaucracy is always producing difference as threat and then subjecting it to violence. It succeeds by exacting violence and making us immune to it by convincing us that the violence is necessary. So, Jesus Christ was not put to death for merely blasphemy, but for sedition, for posing a threat to the state. The religious bureaucracy constructed Jesus Christ's difference as a threat, thereby deserving of violence. Thus, for difference to be different, it must choose love rather than violence.

We must therefore do as Jesus Christ commands. This, again, is the problem with the DEIA movement. It is all about vengeance and violence. We are to assume that violence is necessary for difference to flourish. Those who offend us must be subject to pain and punishment. In this way, the DEIA movement reinforces the idea that violence is necessary and good. This is why this movement is quickly gaining such wide acceptance. We have always believed that violence is necessary and good. ("Spare the rod, spoil the child.") We have also always believed that rules and regulations are necessary and good. As such, the new DEIA movement is in no way a threat to anything. Then again, this was never the plan. It was meant to please and appease, rather than disrupt and transform.

Thirty Two

The Nature of Violence

You put your head down, you keep to yourself. You say nothing to anyone. You neither mess nor meddle with anyone. But still they come for you. In fact, they are always coming for you. Violence needs a target. Someone needs to be deserving of it. If you are different in any way, you are going to stand out. Your difference will make you visible. You will become the target. In this case, your silence makes you visible. Now all that is left to do is to justify the violence. This is what happens when you are of a society with a discursive proclivity for violence. You are always creating and manufacturing targets for your violence, then justifying and rationalizing your violence. There is always violence because there must always be violence.

Unfortunately, what you never recognize is how all your violence is always falling back on you. Your violence reveals your ignorance. Thus, violence can never be an option for those who are wise. Wisdom commands a different response. This would be love. Love is the negation of violence. Whereas violence damages, love affirms. Whereas violence separates, love unites. Whereas violence harms, love heals. This is why Jesus Christ commands us to love, especially those who wrong us. Our redemption resides in love. Only through love can we make a better world that is in every way truly different. Thus, for there to be any possibility of a different world, we must first become different, and this begins with how we treat those who are different.

Thirty Three

THE PROBLEM WITH KNOWLEDGE

From all your violence, it is plain that your knowledge and academic credentials are for nothing. Yet you would still have us believe that our prosperity resides in knowledge. More knowledge will supposedly make everything better. You have now successfully convinced all the world of this. Now the world is obsessed with acquiring more and more knowledge. Ignorance is the enemy we must vanquish. However, you can point to no correlation between knowledge and prosperity. Is the planet facing less peril because of us having more knowledge? Are we facing less of a threat of total annihilation from our own weapons of mass destruction? Are our lives more valuable and meaningful? If so, why then all the addiction, suicide, and mental illness? The reality is that there will always be ignorance. We will never be able to generate all the knowledge we need to end ignorance. On the other hand, ignorance was never our enemy. It is hate, malice, prejudice, vengeance, and violence. As history now makes plain, we can have an abundance of knowledge, and still have all these things. For we are transformed not by how much we know, but by how we live. To save ourselves from hate, malice, prejudice, vengeance, and violence, we must forge the courage and resolve to live differently, meaning to live in ways that impede the rise of these things. This means living like how the prophets command us to live. Indeed, that no prophet left anything in writing is to remind us that our prosperity will only come through our deeds.

Thirty Four

TRANSCENDING GENDER

Personally, I have no interest in gender. I am yet to understand what it has to do with anything important, such as being a just and kind human being. For me, being transgender means that you are transcending gender, getting beyond our obsession with gender, recognizing that we are much more than our biology, much more than the language we are given to describe, experience, and make sense of ourselves. In this regard, I completely support transgenderism. Go forward and live your best life on your own terms and conditions. Help finally rid the world of a notion (gender) that has made for so much subjugation, exploitation, and oppression.

However, now I am learning that, for many in the transgender community, being transgender means something quite different. Rather than transcending gender, it is about reifying gender. The goal is simply to be of a different gender, or another kind of gender. But gender remains front and center. Many simply want to declare, "Now I am happy. I am finally in the right body, of the correct gender." Being of the wrong gender is supposedly the problem. It is the cause of all your misery.

The Buddha says that "mind is everything." That the mind is everything means that our minds shape our experiencing and understanding of everything. Any kind of misery or turmoil originates in our minds. Thus, if we are to save ourselves from any kind of misery or turmoil, we must attend to our minds. For the mind, rather than the body, is everything. However, for many in the transgender community, the body is everything. Only by changing the configuration of the body will peace be found.

Buddhism also warns us about becoming obsessed with form, like the human body. Yes, there is always form, and form can be beautiful. However, form decays and perishes. Instead, Buddhism, like Hinduism and Jainism, teaches us to value spirit rather than form. Spirit endures, transcends. Many Buddhist practices are about reminding us that form is nothing. Form is also susceptible to desire and attachment, of being ruled by the senses. Desire is the beginning of human misery. Thus, any desire, including the desire to be of a different form, in this case a different body or gender, would conflict with all that Buddhism teaches about the origins of human misery.

In *The Yoga Sutras of Patanjali*, there is a nice discussion about how our suffering originates in our ignorance regarding the non-Self and the Self:

> What is the Self and what is the non-Self? The Self is the eternal, never-changing One. It is always everywhere as the very basic substance. All things are actually nothing but the Self, but in our ignorance, we see them as different objects. Thus, we take the changing appearances to be the unchanging truth. When something changes, it can't be the Self. For example, our own bodies are changing every second. Yet we take the body to be our Self; and, speaking in terms of it, we say, "I am hungry" or "I am physically challenged;" "I am Black" or "I am white." These are all just the conditions and qualities of the body . . . If the body aches, then the body is sick, not you. Whenever we forget this truth, we are involved in the non-Self, the basic ignorance. (p. 82)

We are also to "remember that the body is not the experiencer. Life is experienced by the mind through the body. The body is only a vehicle or instrument."

(p. 92) Again, the point being that we are much more than the shapes and configurations of our bodies. Much more than Black or white, male or female, homosexual or heterosexual. We should focus on what makes us more rather than less.

Further, a key teaching that forms the foundation of Buddhism says that there is always suffering, but our suffering is always of our making, either through desire or attachment. In other words, our suffering does not come from the nature or configuration of our bodies. It comes from our minds, our way of viewing and understanding something. But this we can change, and this is what we must change to end our misery and suffering. Thus, from the perspective of Buddhism, or one humble interpretation of Buddhism, no changing of our body or gender will ever end your suffering. Our suffering originates in our minds rather than in our bodies.

Thirty Five

JOY AND PAIN

Now I understand. Cruelty is born of pain. This truth is no longer abstract to me. So now I am no longer angry at you. No longer puzzled by all your cruelty, even with all your academic credentials. For I always knew that your academic credentials, like mine, meant nothing in terms of wisdom. Being wise and being knowledge are two different things. For what is the value of any amount of knowledge that does nothing to make us kinder and gentler? That is, what is the value of any knowledge that gives us neither joy nor enlightenment?

So again, I am no longer angry at you. Now all I feel is empathy and compassion for you. I hope you can eventually find a way out of your pain and cruelty. Buddhism teaches that our misery is always of our own making. So just as much as we make our suffering, just as just we can do the opposite. But first we must own the fact that we make our own suffering. There is therefore a path out of your suffering. You should take it.

I wish you well.

Thirty Six

REDEFINING COMMUNICATION

When two Black folks are speaking and one asks, "You feel me?," and the other responds, "I feel you.," in that moment Black folks are upending everything in communication and rhetorical studies. Black folks are suggesting that communication is ultimately about what is felt rather than what is spoken or written. How we can feel more deeply and intensely should concern us most.

Of course, many would claim that communication and rhetorical studies already takes affect seriously. However, when Black folks speak about being felt, this is much deeper than simply a matter of affect. It is about being intuitively understood at a deep level, beyond the level of words, meanings, and messages. For Black folks, communication is about vulnerability. It is much more than opening our minds to each other. It is also about opening our hearts and souls to each other.

Thirty Seven

INEQUALITY

S ome ideas refuse to die. Regardless of how hard we try to vanquish them with empirical or historical evidence, they endure. One such idea is human inequality — that certain groups are inherently superior to others, and this distinction is intellectually and morally observable and measurable. Of course, many contend that this idea endures because it is simply true. We are merely trying to vanquish it because we dislike what it represents. As such, the problem is us. Because we cannot deal with this supposed truth, we want to suppress it and destroy the reputation of those what advance it. In this case, both have probably occurred. Indeed, many who oppose this idea do openly call for the suppression of this idea by any means necessary. We are told that allowing this idea to be discussed, especially on college campuses, gives it credibility and, in doing so, keeps it alive. But I beg to differ. We get pass things by confronting them honestly and transparently. Just like how only light can drive out darkness, only knowledge can drive out ignorance.

Those who claim that inequality is real contend that this inequality is both moral and intellectual. Those who are supposedly superior act one way, and those who are inferior act another. We are to assume that being superior represents a moral and intellectual order that is outside of time and space. It supposedly has nothing to do with ideology and history. It is supposedly universally definable and observable. However, history challenges this claim. For if those who have been ruling the world are supposedly the best and brightest, as the cream supposedly rises to the top, then do over 350 years of slavery, Black Codes, and Jim Crow represent a superior moral and intellectual order? If so, superior to what exactly? Also, does the creation and proliferation of weapons of mass destruction, which now threaten us all, represent a superior moral and intellectual order? Again, if so, compared to what? That is, how would a world devoid of these weapons represent an inferior moral and intellectual order? Further, how does our destruction of the planet represent a superior moral and intellectual order? Where is the superiority in our destruction of our only habitat? What can those who are supposedly inferior do that is worse? Moreover, what is morally and intellectually about World War I and II, the most destructive wars the world has even seen? Also, what is morally and intellectually superior about our consumerism and materialism, especially when the planet is now running out of natural resources? What could those who are morally and intellectually inferior do that is more destructive? Further, how does mass incarceration reflect a superior moral and intellectual order? Finally, what science affirms the claim that those who are supposedly morally and intellectually superior are living more valuable and meaningful lives?

There is nothing inherently wrong with there being variation in human abilities and capabilities. In fact, being blessed with different talents seems cool. However, those who are pushing the idea of human inequality are saying something quite different. They are saying human inequality is about the distinction between superior and inferior groups. In other words, human variation is about inequality rather than diversity. Thus, what should supposedly matter to us most in terms of public policy is recognizing our inequality rather than our diversity.

However, human beings are first and foremost interpretive beings. We interpret everything, and because our experiences and circumstances will always be different, we will always interpret things differently. So, for one group, being better at something can mean something important, and for another it can mean nothing. We can have human variation without human inequality. Human inequality represents a specific ideology and epistemology. It says that a certain group is attaching certain meanings to different things that advantage and privilege certain people and disadvantage and deprivilege others. The fact that I score high on a standardized test can simply mean that I score high on a test. That the test will supposedly predict that I will do well in something only means that I will do well in something. To claim that my score on a test makes me morally and intellectually superior is an act of interpretation. Again, there is always interpretation. However, our interpretations are always serving different masters. No interpretation is ever outside of ideology.

Those who champion human inequality want to suppress the fact that our descriptions are nothing but our interpretations. Before we can study and make theory about anything, like intelligence, we must first begin with a definition of that thing, which is an act of interpretation. Interpretive beings are subjective beings, meaning that all our definitions and descriptions reflect our values, beliefs, and desires. From an interpretive standpoint, it is never about what is real, but rather what is real to whom, and whose interests are best served by what is supposedly so. As such, when human variation is interpreted as inequality rather than diversity, whose interest is best served? Interpretive beings are also political beings. We are always contesting and challenging each other's different descriptions and interpretations. But again, this is what the champions of human inequality wish to suppress. We are to assume that human inequality is an objective fact. It has nothing to do with politics, and thereby nothing to do with power. It is just a fact of nature that we would be wise to simply accept.

We can interpret human variation in many things. Viewing it in terms of inequality is merely our thing. It works for us in terms of legitimizing the world that serves the interests of some. We like the idea of believing that our success is purely of nature running its course. We are successful because we are superior. Our success supposedly has nothing to do with anything else. It is simply a matter of the crème rising to the top. Success is supposedly a natural process. Those who are superior will always rise to the top and acquire all the rewards and privileges that come with doing so. Conversely, those who are presumably inferior will fall to the bottom and get nothing. Such is supposedly the order of things, and only fools believe and pretend otherwise. Thus, those who defend human inequality also tend to defend the status quo. Moreover, those who defend human inequality contend that human inequality is best for all. Those who are supposedly inferior are better off when ruled by the best and brightest. Also, those who defend human inequality claim that excellence can only come from allowing inequality to flourish. To interfere with the natural order of things is to promote a mediocrity that is of no use to anyone in the long term. However, this is how oppression begins, in the oppressor trying to convince the oppressed that the status quo equally serves all groups, and thus they should never do anything to threaten it. But, of course, such is never the case.

Human inequality is about resources. It is about who is presumably deserving of more resources and who is deserving of less. For instance, champions of human inequality often ask: why should certain people go to college who would probably be better off, based on test scores, going to a vocational school and becoming, say, a plumber or carpenter? Human inequality is also about opportunity. Again, champions of human inequality often ask: why give those who are supposedly inferior special admission to elite schools that they are intellectually incapable of exploiting? Is the world truly better served by doctors who do poorly medical schools? In short, defenders of human inequality believe that a good society is efficient. It uses and allocates resources and opportunities efficiently. Through standardized testing we determine what resources and opportunities each person gets and deserves. A society that functions efficiently supposedly works best for all. Also, a society works best when every component is in the right place and performing its function to the best of its ability. We supposedly cannot all be transmissions. Machines also need many small components to do a lot of small things. We should all know our place and be at peace with it. But whose metaphor is this, society as machine? No doubt, human beings are metaphorical beings. But no metaphor simply drops from the sky. Our metaphors reflect our worldviews, all the forces that shape and guide our minds. When I adopt your metaphors, I am ultimately adopting your mind. Your worldview is now my worldview. As such, in order to look at the world differently, I must abandon your metaphors. Diversity means that our minds run on different metaphors.

Viewing society as a machine assumes that our potential is observable and measurable. Through testing, our function and position can be known. That is, our potential is set by nature. However, neuroplasticity is now revealing that our minds can change in profound ways by physically changing how we live. In other words, rather than static, our minds are dynamic. Confining us to one function or location, as a machine demands, impedes the development of our minds. Our minds need environments that offer high levels of tension and disruption. We should be forced and challenged to live in ways that stretch the limits of our being. Also, viewing us as simply measurable cogs downplays our complexity. There is no doubt a biological dimension to the human experience. However, there are also emotional, existential, historical, spiritual, intellectual, relational, and ecological dimensions as well. Our potentiality is the sum of all these dimensions, meaning that there is no way to reliably predict the limits of our potentiality. That IQ supposedly has predictive capability is only because IQ is predicting what the makers of IQ deem important. Finally, the problem with viewing society as machine is the loss of human freedom, and all the diversity that this freedom represents. The purpose of measuring us is to control us. Your test score will determine what resources and privileges you will get. Hierarchy is supposedly inevitable. For defenders of human inequality, hierarchies are really hierarchies of competence and excellence. However, history tells a different story of hierarchy. History reveals that where we find hierarchies, especially elaborate hierarchies, we are all but certain to find human misery. The reason is that hierarchy impedes the autonomy or freedom vital to becoming fully human. In depriving us of autonomy, it strips us of the responsibility we need to own the condition of our lives. In being released from being responsible for our actions and deci-sions, we become reckless and promiscuous. We do silly and cowardly things. Thus, rather than fostering human dignity, hierarchies do the opposite. So, the fact that hierarchies appear natural does not mean they are moral or eco-logical. We need freedom because it promotes responsibility. Only through responsibility is human dignity possible.

Thirty Eight

DEATH AND DYING

I cannot imagine a more powerful force than death. This is probably why we do everything to avoid it. To reckon with it requires enormous strength. For death is powerful because it is meant to destroy, but in a positive rather than a negative way. For instance, death destroys our delusions, thereby helping to focus on what is real and important. Death blows up our attachments, such as our attachment to the past that stops us from valuing the present. Death disabuses us of ideas that are no longer useful or valuable. In short, death gives us clarity. It releases us from intellectual, emotional, existential, and spiritual bondage. Moreover, death makes courage possible. Courage is about living in the face of death, being unafraid to die. It is about the strength to die, both figuratively and literally. This is why nearly all religious scriptures speak of death in terms of rebirth and redemption. Only through death we are born anew. There is no life without death, no death without life.

So, you want to know if you are truly living, then look at how much dying, if any, you are doing. What and how many things are you no longer valuing, believing, or doing? Are you, for instance, allowing past grudges and mistakes to die? There is no doubt many ways to die. But only in dying we will find the courage to truly live.

Faith says that I will be fine. I will find life in death. I will neither be forsaken nor abandoned. But I will never recklessly or selfishly choose death. Life is sacred and I am happy to be alive. However, I will never choose to live as a coward, devoid of faith and courage. We hear that faith is about believing in things unseen. It is a nice definition. For me, however, faith is about our resolve to do as the prophets command us to do. Is the person willing to die for the sake of love and justice? Is the person willing to lose all the things of this world? Faith speaks to character. If death is the price for doing what the prophets command, then I am ready to die. For again, I will be fine.

But make no mistake, in our world, dying is hard. We do almost everything to avoid it. Such is the nature and purpose of materialism and professionalism. Just look at all the things you will lose if you choose to die. You will be shamed for publishing your own book. It will never be reviewed anywhere. It will receive no award. It will do nothing for your case for tenure and promotion. Thus, many would ask why be a fool and publish your book? Why jeopardize your career like that? However, I do it because Hinduism, Buddhism, and Christianity all teach that I should do nothing for any kind of reward. I therefore do it as a spiritual practice. It is about dying, refusing to be controlled by my desires and becoming attached to a world made by man rather God. So, in choosing to publish my own book, I am choosing to die so I can live. I am choosing detachment rather attachment. That is, in choosing death, I am choosing liberation, releasing myself of all the delusions in academe that for too long have made for my intellectual and spiritual bondage. For only in death, we are free, truly free.

Thirty Nine

ORDER/CHAOS

*I*f you value order, you believe hierarchy is necessary. You believe that rules and regulations make order possible. You also believe that we should always be devising better ways to enact and maintain order. Further, you believe order is necessary because human beings have a proclivity for mayhem and mischief. Consequently, without order, chaos will rise and destroy us. Thus, for progress and prosperity to be possible, hierarchy is necessary.

This idea about hierarchy is foundational to western civilization. We hear again and again that hierarchy is both natural and necessary. Supposedly, only fools believe otherwise. We are told that hierarchy reflects human inequality. Those who are supposedly superior rise to the top, and those who are inferior fall to the bottom. Consequently, those who are superior craft the rules and regulations, and those who are inferior follow the rules and regulations.

However, rather than cultivating order, hierarchy cultivates deviancy and dysfunctionality. It does so by separating us from the consequences of our actions. In other words, hierarchy releases us from responsibility for the consequences of our actions by no longer making our actions ours. If our actions are no longer ours, then we cannot be responsible for them. So, I did what I did because you ordered or commanded me to do so. How can I now be responsible for the consequences that followed? All your rules and regulations made it all but impossible for me to do otherwise.

This is the perverse nature of hierarchy. It releases us from responsibility for the condition of our lives. There is nothing much for us to figure out. No consequences to reckon with. There are now rules and regulations, norms and conventions, for almost everything. Case in point, our schools have already determined what classes we need to take and when. That we never have to figure anything out means we never struggle and persevere. We just need to follow all the rules and regulations, norms and conventions, and we will be fine. But all our neuroses and psychoses now reveal that we are anything but fine. We are institutionalized. We cannot function without hierarchy. We now do need rules and regulations for everything. So, in schools we are doing exactly as we are ordered and commanded to do. However, we are learning nothing. There is no kind of transformation happening from all our learning and studying. It is all a great waste of time. But it is worse than this. All our schooling is harming us. Besides the institutionalization, there is the alienation, the separation of being from doing. We are, besides learning nothing, becoming nothing. It is our increasing alienation that is escalating our neuroses and psychoses. Alienation paralyzes us by making us weak and cowardly. It stops us from acting boldly and courageously by robbing us of the drive necessary to do so. We are constantly afraid of what will happen if we were to violate any rule or regulation. After all, violating rules and regulations is meant to bring pain. The goal is to make your life unpleasant for refusing to submit and conform. Regardless of whether the rule is fair or unfair is secondary. All that matters is our submitting and conforming. Thus, the struggle to save ourselves from the ravages of institutionalization and alienation is hard.

Then there is the infantilization that hierarchy produces. To follow is to obey and conform. Rules and regulations singularize and homogenize. Hierarchy succeeds by smashing human diversity. That I must obey and conform means that I must ultimately believe that doing so is good and even necessary. It also means that I should trust those who are making all the rules and regulations I must follow and obey. Supposedly, these people are deserving of this power. Supposedly, these people are even better than me. Supposedly, these people represent a cognitive elite with a superior IQ and intelligence. We are therefore to always listen to the experts. We should make nothing of the fact that the supposed experts are nearly always wrong. What matters is the idea of the experts, certain people having the authority to control our lives, and thus being responsible for our lives. For with experts, nothing needs to be figured out by us. We merely have to submit and conform. But again, doing so infantilizes us by blocking us from struggling and even failing. We gain nothing from internalizing the belief that we are incapable of doing extraordinary things. However, no hierarchy can succeed without us internalizing this belief. Thus, rather than excellence, the hallmark of hierarchy is mediocrity — large groups of human beings lacking the courage, fortitude, and discipline to act boldly and imaginatively.

So yes, the ubiquity of hierarchy would make it seem natural. This is supposedly what human beings do in every region around the world. However, that something seems natural does not mean it is moral and ecological. Hierarchy seems natural only because it is easy. It requires no courage to follow, obey, and conform. However, easy never ends well for us. History reminds us again and again that hierarchy is always at the center of all great human evils. There would have been no slavery, no segregation, no World War I and II, no Holocaust, without hierarchy. Human beings are designed to struggle, to become better from struggling. Through struggle we enlarge our sense of everything. In other words, through struggle we become moral, better versions of ourselves. Thus, in releasing us of struggle, hierarchy impedes our moral development. Such again is the perversion of hierarchy. You rise in any hierarchy by obeying, submitting, conforming, and then demanding that those below you do likewise if they wish to succeed like you.

But to live our best lives we must become more than moral. We must also become ecological — recognize that we must live in harmony with other organic beings that share our spaces and resources. But hierarchy makes this impossible. A hierarchy succeeds by making us believe that we are fundamentally biological beings. We are "survival machines" doing the bidding of "selfish genes." Hierarchy is supposedly a natural arrangement between "survival machines" of different skills and talents. Its origins are supposedly evolutionary. Our life, even prosperity, is dependent on us devising creative ways to get along with others. If we cannot survive by being strong, then we must do so by other means. This means being able to persuade, manipulate, coerce, and even seduce. Thus, from a hierarchical perspective, we succeed by always looking out for our own self-interest. However, from an ecological perspective, we succeed by looking out for the interest of others. This is why so many in biology are yet to properly explain altruism. In a world of competition and selfishness, altruism makes no sense. However, from an ecological perspective, altruism makes plenty sense. It represents an ecological sensibility, a recognition that the whole is always greater than the sum of all the parts in any system.

Order is a narrative. In this narrative, order is the protagonist. It heroically saves us from the ravages of chaos. In doing so, order supposedly makes progress and prosperity possible. But as with any narrative, there are always omissions, distortions, fabrications, and exaggerations. In other words, in this popular order narrative, chaos is getting a bad deal. It is being demonized. We are to assume that order and chaos are separate things that are against each other. Order can only rise by vanquishing chaos. We are also to assume that chaos, or what we perceive as chaos, has no redeeming value. It supposedly contributes nothing to the flourishing of life. But, of course, chaos theory now tells us differently. Chaos and order are bound up with each other. If we want a productive, constructive, and generative order, then such an order must come from chaos. Hierarchy assumes that order must be imposed on us through rules and regulations. However, chaos theory now tells us that for order to be possible, responsibility is necessary. We must be compelled to reckon with the consequences of our actions. Never must we be released from doing so. Compelling us to be responsible for our actions is therefore much more than creating a productive, constructive, and generative order. It is about pushing us to become moral and ecological. Indeed, rather than being necessary to make progress and prosperity possible, order is a byproduct of us becoming moral and ecological. So, whereas hierarchy assumes that order must come first, it should come last in reality. But again, actions have consequences. That hierarchy now shapes nearly every facet of our lives means that we are devoid of significant moral and ecological development. Consequently, our neuroses and psychoses are increasingly many. Our addictions are no less so. Any kind of chaos or disruption causes us all manner of anxiety and torment. We are increasingly intellectually and emotionally fragile. Our narcissism is out of control.

We now have an abundance of knowledge. Never before has the world had so much knowledge. However, all this knowledge is in no way translating to us living full and meaningful lives. But such again is the consequence of hierarchy. It robs us of the ability to problem solve. For what is the value of being learned if we are unable to use all that we are learning to live richer lives? In fact, what is the value of any world that has rules and regulations for everything, but full of people who cannot live independently and creatively? Yet such is the world that is now upon us.

Fourty

POWER

History teaches us a lot about power.

I.   There is always power. It is always circulating, always shaping and guiding how a system works and behaves.
II.   Power begins in the ego. We want what we want.
III. Those who have power will use, seduce, or take advantage of any excuse or circumstance to acquire more of it.
IV.   Those who acquire it will never return it without a struggle.
V.   There is always resistance to power.
VI.   Those who desire power will always desire more of it.
VII. Finally, power is never evenly distributed. For some to have more of it, others must have less of it. Consequently, no system is ever evenly influenced by all members.

What then is the moral of the story? We should always be mindful that every system is always being shaped and influenced in ways that better serve some rather than others. Nothing is inherently wrong about this. But we should always be mindful of how a system is being shaped and whose interest is best being served.

Fourty One

A Theory of Revolution

We are now of a world full of egotism, dogmatism, and narcissism. Self-righteousness is the new normal. We are always being offended, outraged, and traumatized. We are beyond right and wrong. Now when you are wrong, you are evil. You deserve to be canceled, shamed, and brutalized. There must be no redemption for you. Never call us again. We want nothing to do with you. Crawl under a rock and die. In fact, this is how the learned and educated now demand we treat you. To treat you differently is supposedly to normalize your offensive action. We would then be complicit in your offensiveness. After all, what you did was so egregious that nothing less than your full banishment would do. That you said something without any hate or malice counts for nothing. Intent supposedly has nothing to do with anything. We demand vengeance. You must be destroyed. Mercy and forgiveness, grace and generosity, mean nothing to you. However, what you are missing is the fact that mercy and forgiveness, grace and generosity, are meant for us, to stop us from becoming ugly by doing ugly things to others.

Biology now tells us that understanding genes requires understanding environments. Our genes and environments shape and influence each other. Psychology now tells us that we cannot understand mind without understanding how we live. Our minds shape how we live and how we live shapes our minds. Similarly, communicology tells us we cannot understand meaning without understanding context. Meaning and context are inseparable. We should refrain from believing that we can reliably know what another person means by uttering certain words. A lot of communication is about guessing, approximating, and triangulating. Compounding this reality is the fact that meaning is in us. We ultimately determine what things mean. However, because our backgrounds and experiences will always be different, the meanings we individually attach to things will always be different. In short, because of the ambiguous nature of communication, grace and generosity are vital for communication to succeed. On the other hand, when we practice grace and generosity, we become beautiful, and in turn contribute to the making of a beautiful world. This is how communication is constitutive. In making us beautiful, communication makes the world beautiful. Thus, within communication resides a theory of revolution and redemption, meaning that there is a path to a better world. However, realizing this world will demand of us first transforming ourselves. We will have to live differently, such as refraining from destroying others.

Fourty Two

Excellence

*Y*our standards of excellence have nothing to do with excellence. After all, there is no objective notion of excellence in your standards of excellence, meaning no idea of excellence that is outside of history and ideology. Instead, your standards of excellence are meant for us, for you to dominate and colonize us. We are to believe you are superior to us. You should nr the arbiter of excellence. In you knowing what is excellent, you supposedly also know who is excellent, and, consequently, who and what is mediocre.

This is why you are increasingly claiming that excellence is under attack. Supposedly, because we cannot meet your standards of excellence, we want to destroy them. Supposedly, this is how mediocre people behave. We destroy that which we cannot uphold. You claim that the death of excellence will be the death of all of us. Who, after all, benefits from mediocre doctors, engineers, and teachers? As such, you believe that we should all now rally, regardless of race, creed, and gender, and defend prevailing standards of excellence with all our might.

Excellence is your new weapon against human diversity. You are no doubt afraid of all the human diversity that is increasingly upon you. You fear this diversity will end your rule, your civilization. In many ways, you have good reason to be afraid. Your rule has been oppressive and destructive. There is much blood on your hands. For you, excellence is about protecting the integrity of your institutions. You know full well that if your institutions were to fall, your civilization would end. So again, your standards of excellence have nothing to do with excellence. You are about protecting your institutions, and, in turn, your supposed right to dominate and colonize. Still, this is a clever move, accusing us of being hostile to excellence. It is another way of fostering the impression that we are nothing but savages. We supposedly have no appreciation of the demands of excellence. We are either incapable or simply unwilling to put in all the hard work and discipline that excellence demands.

By invoking excellence, you succeed in conflating diversity with mediocrity. Now you can claim that you are really against mediocrity rather than diversity. It is supposedly mediocrity that threatens us. Let us end mediocrity by upholding our prevailing standards of excellence, meaning your standards of excellence that have nothing to do with excellence. Again, clever move. Well-played indeed. You never have to account for the supposed excellence in your standards of excellence. But what exactly is this excellence? Where do we find it in over 350 years of slavery and Jim Crow? Where is it in the Holocaust and over 2,000 years of Jewish persecution? Where is it in our destruction of the planet? Or in World War I and II? Where is it in our creation and proliferation of weapons mass destruction? Indeed, how did you miraculously come to a model of excellence that is outside of time and space, history and ideology?

The reality is that your standards of excellence are purely of your own making, born of everything you believe, value, and desire. When we uphold your standards of excellence, we are upholding everything you believe, value, and desire. Nothing, of course, is inherently wrong with this. However, if we are going to do this, then we should compel you to prove or demonstrate that your standards of excellence represent an excellence that we should want to embrace and emulate. But this is where your cleverness ends. You can provide no such evidence. History lends for no such case. This is what you are afraid of, us coming to recognize that there is no excellence in your standards of excellence. It is all ideology, power, and politics. Excellence is an ideograph, a tool you are using to cultivate, promote, and normalize your ideology. This is why you are now fighting to preserve this ideograph. If it was to fall, this would undermine the hegemony of your ideology. However, it is much more than history that is against you. The order of the natural world is against you. Your standards of excellence are contrary to how the world defines and goes about promoting excellence.

There is nothing arbitrary about excellence in the natural world. Excellence means flourishing to the best of your ability. It is about realizing your full potential. This is why evolution is such an integral element in life. Evolution demands excellence. Through excellence we flourish. Excellence is the hallmark of life. It is what makes life wondrous. This is how we now know that the world damns your model of excellence. It produces nothing wondrous, nothing life affirming. Instead, all we get is destruction, misery, and torment. You claim that we oppose excellence. However, what we oppose is the mediocrity that your model of excellence represents. We know full well that nothing good comes from mediocrity. If we are to flourish, we must be excellent. We must strive to live in ways that tap our full potential, which means living in ways that allow us to have all the resources we need to flourish. After all, how are we to flourish without the resources necessary to do so? The natural world teaches us that excellence is ecological. We become excellent by pushing and challenging others to be excellent, which includes helping others acquire all the resources they need to become so.

Fourty Three

TRUTH

The first question is the oldest, what is truth? However, I want to begin with a different question, why should truth matter? Why do we even need to have it? Is it always necessary? Is it always good and positive? Do we always gain from having it? Finally, how did we come to believe that truth was something we need, and that regardless of the costs and consequences, we should have it?

For sure, truth is by no means a bed of roses. First, truth impedes communication. Communication is now about establishing the truth rather than finding the truth. Such, of course, is the nature of the US legal system. It is about determining who is telling the truth rather than finding the truth. Second, truth impedes diversity. We commonly assume that truth is singular rather than plural. There can only be one truth. If what you have is different to what I have, which is supposedly the truth, you have a problem. Third, truth impedes humility. Why should I be humble if I have the truth? Finally, truth impedes community. Community assumes a common truth. "We hold these truths to be self-evident." Thus, people holding conflicting truths supposedly threatens community.

However, there is never one truth. Life is about perspective. In fact, all human beings have is a perspective, and different perspectives make for different truths. We can also claim that no human can command a final and perfect truth. For example, no human being will ever know who made God, or what was the bang that set off the Big Bang, or what happens after death, or what, if any, is the meaning of life? We can also claim that truth is unnecessary. We can live good lives without it. Indeed, does the world need more truth, or more love, more compassion, more mercy, more kindness, more forgiveness, more generosity, more grace? What then is all the commotion about truth about?

We have one question still to answer. Why do we remain obsessed with truth? I believe that truth, if there is such a thing, belongs to the realm of gods, if there is such a thing. In other words, we are obsessed with the idea of truth because we would like to believe that we can be gods. We can therefore do as gods supposedly have the power to do. Thus, for us, truth means power, as in the power to transform the world. Those who command it are powerful. So, nothing is wrong with, say, love and mercy, but neither gives us the power that truth supposedly does. In the end, truth is for us. It has nothing to do with the world. It is something we put into the world rather than find in the world.

Fourty Four

No Power in Words

*W*e say again and again that words have power. We appear convinced that this supposed truth was be given to us by gods. We even make policy on this supposed truth. Say the wrong in the wrong place and for sure you will be either canceled, investigated, suspended, expelled, or terminated. However, no one is yet to tell us exactly how words came to have power. What is the name of that process? Is it empirically verifiable? We are merely to assume that such is the case.

Yet, for all we claim about words having power, we do not really believe this. After all, soon after claiming that words have power, we say in the next breath that words mean nothing to us. We want actions. We want deeds.

The reality is that we like the idea of words having power. For words to have power, we must give them power. That is, we must give away our power to words. However, when we give away our power to anything, we also give away responsibility for our lives. So, the more power words have, the less responsibility we have for our lives. This is why the Bible warns us about worshiping false gods. Also, do your words hurt me, or do I allow your words to hurt me? It is, of course, the latter. But to own this, I must own responsibility for my

life, and this is hard. This is why we give away our power. This is why we create false gods. Responsibility is hard. Responsibility means owning the consequences of our actions. We will offer no excuses. However, as much as we like
to believe that words have power, such will never be the case. It will remain
nothing but a delusion. Also, this delusion can do nothing to suppress our
hypocrisy in terms of preferring deeds to words. In the end, we ae all entitled
to our delusions. But delusions have consequences.

Fourty Five

Science and Knowledge

It is a fool's errand. I am referring to our ambition and determination to strip the world of its ambiguity, complexity, and mystery. We believe that we must do this for the sake of acquiring the knowledge we supposedly need to evolve and thrive. We therefore believe that knowledge is about demystifying and extracting things. For us, knowledge is about light, and ignorance is about darkness. Indeed, for us, inquiry is about shedding light, removing the darkness. Consequently, for us, progress is about generating knowledge and displacing ignorance. In other words, for us, life is a struggle between knowledge and ignorance, light and darkness. Winning this struggle means generating as much knowledge as possible. We must always be producing more and more knowledge and preparing more and more people to do so. Again, the more knowledge we can generate, supposedly the more ignorance we can displace. Who, after all, wants to return to the "Dark Age" where we were ruled by ignorance?

This is where science enters the picture. Science supposedly represents the most reliable means to generate all the knowledge we need. Science will mine the world for knowledge, especially for those nuggets that we subjectively judge to be more valuable than others. It will deconstitute the world and lay it bare. It will unlock and reveal all the world's secrets. The goal of science "is simple. It is a complete understanding of the universe, why it is as it is and why it exists at all." For us, science is a mining operation. Knowledge comes from extraction.

We are to believe, of course, that science is objective. It is merely an enterprise we use to generate knowledge. There is supposedly no ideology and politics. But this is false. Again, science assumes that the world is of a conflict between light and darkness, knowledge and ignorance. The more knowledge we can generate, the more progress we will have. This belief, among others, made for the invention of science and our believing that science represents the most effective operation human beings ever devised to generate knowledge. For us, ignorance is the negation of knowledge. We must have knowledge to evolve and thrive. Without it, we are damned. We also believe that science not merely gives us more knowledge, but more valuable and important knowledge, meaning gold nuggets of knowledge.

We therefore cannot allow the world to have its complexity, ambiguity, and mystery. To do so is supposedly to allow ignorance to stand. Progress demands that we are always deconstituting the world, mining it for all its knowledge. There is supposedly nothing in the world that science cannot deconstitute and lay bare. But as the Bible says, we will know a tree by its fruits. In this case, what does the world's current condition reveal about our progress and prosperity narrative? Is all the knowledge we are producing and generating making the world better? Can our progress and prosperity be found in the Holocaust? World War I and II? What about our contamination and pollution of all the world's oceans, rivers, and streams? Or the ecological peril that is now upon as the glaciers melt and the oceans warm? Or the explosion of addiction and mental illness? Again, where is the progress and prosperity that was to come from all the knowledge that science is busy producing and generating?

Viewing science in terms of mining is an apt metaphor. In the process of mining the world for metals and minerals, we destroy it. No different to what happens in science when we experiment on animals. Also, like science, mining assumes that the destruction is necessary. It is supposedly the only way we will acquire the metals and minerals we need to prosper. Also, just like how mining assumes that we need metals and minerals to prosper, science assumes that we need knowledge to prosper. In both cases, we must forget that we attach meaning to things. Precious metals are us attaching meaning to certain metals. The value of these metals comes from us. Science is no different. We must forget that we attach value and meaning to the knowledge science generates. Finally, like mining, science assumes that violence is necessary to create something that is supposedly valuable. We must pry the world open to achieve knowledge. We must always be extracting and dissecting. In this way, science is violence. It is us trying to find more and more powerful means to force the world to give up its secrets.

Metaphors and narratives form each other. In our narrative, we are achieving progress and prosperity. We are successfully displacing the world's darkness. We are supposedly becoming more and more enlightened, and in the process achieving dominion over the world. Never before has the world had so much knowledge. We must therefore credit science for our progress. We should also credit the civilization that give us science, and the people who give us this civilization. We supposedly owe them our full gratitude. But now the chickens are coming home to roost. We are increasingly being forced to recognize that we will never conquer the world's darkness. Most of the world is made up of dark matter and dark energy. No amount of science will ever penetrate all this dark matter and dark energy. Again, this is a fool's errand. However, it is much more than merely so. It is destructive. It has distorted our relationship to both knowledge and ignorance. We believe that knowledge and ignorance, like light and darkness, are separate things that conflict with each other. But this is false. There is no knowledge that is devoid of ignorance, no ignorance devoid of knowledge. Rather than oppositional, knowledge and ignorance, like light and darkness, are dialectical. Both are bound up with each other. However, rather than the absence of knowledge, ignorance means humility. Its purpose is to remind us of all we will never know. In other words, ignorance makes for awe and wonder. That we will know where life came from is about awe and wonder. What we claim to know will always reflect our limits. By instilling humility, ignorance impedes violence. It stops us from believing that our truths are final and perfect, and thus beyond criticism.

Ultimately, what is going to save us is us recognizing that we need to stop cultivating violence. The violence we are now waging in the name of science, like any other kind of violence, is only falling back on us. This is why so much of the knowledge that science is producing is doing nothing good for us. What the world demands of us is harmony, us coming to peace with the world's boundless ambiguity, complexity, and mystery. We achieve harmony by recognizing that this ambiguity, complexity, and mystery is a blessing. It should be embraced rather than attacked. We are better off when we are compelled to be humble. Humility impedes our worse instincts and impulses. It stops violence. It reminds us that the good of life is found in how we live rather than in how much we know. Humility, like compassion and forgiveness, makes us beautiful, and this is what ultimately matters. What is the value of possessing an abundance of knowledge if it does nothing to make us beautiful? All the prophets tell us that the goal of life is to become beautiful. This is where our redemption resides. To become beautiful involves making others beautiful and, ultimately, making the world beautiful. We need both light and darkness, knowledge and ignorance, to become beautiful. If light gives us clarity, darkness gives us humility. If light gives us answers, darkness gives us questions. Thus, rather than focusing on whether our knowledge is true or false, we should be focusing on whether it is valuable. Is it transforming us for the better? Is it making us beautiful?

That the world's ambiguity, complexity, and mystery is boundless means that we are also boundless. There are no limits to how beautiful we can become. There are therefore no limits to how much we can imagine and experience. Thus, only in such a world we are truly blessed.

Fourty Six

METAPHORS

We are metaphorical beings. We use metaphors to explain and understand. For us in the western world, war is our popular metaphor, which reveals a lot. Indeed, metaphors come from our ideologies and do the bidding of our ideologies. This is why ideology is important. In shaping our metaphors, our ideology ultimately shapes how we frame and relate to things.

Viewing science in terms of mining is revealing in many ways. We get to visualize the process. We see science as an extractive process searching for gems of knowledge. We see all the machines that science now uses, such as the superconductor collider, to lay the world bare. We see the constant drilling, the endless experiments, to deconstitute the world. We also see the many failures, the many mines, which will produce nothing valuable. Moreover, we see the destruction that will come from all the mining and experimenting. Mining will make the world ugly. The sites will become eyesores. There will be pollution and contamination of streams. Mountains and forests will be no more. Only scars and wounds to the earth will remain after all the metals and minerals have been extracted.

With science, the destruction will be no different. A lot of animals will have to die for us to get the gems of knowledge we desire. However, this is merely one kind of destruction that comes from science. There is the destruction that comes with deconstituting things. We destroy the relationship between things when we forcefully divide and separate things. Things that are meant to be understood ecologically are now seen oppositionally. In communication studies, we separate meaning from ambiguity, communication from confusion, speech from silence, speaker from listener, message from medium. These divisions and separations distort our understanding of things. For again, what we lose is the relationship between things. Indeed, the most important relationship we lose is our own relationship to things. Our values and beliefs shape how we frame, perceive, and make sense of things. Objectivity is a delusion. Precious metals and minerals are nothing but our attaching our own beliefs and values to things we deem to be valuable. What we do in science is no different. We are always making decisions about what knowledge is important and valuable, and thus what knowledge is deserving of publication in our most prestigious scholarly journals. Nothing about this process is devoid of ideology and politics. Mining is no different. In the end, both mining and science would like us to believe that both extractive operations are simply necessary to get what we need from the world to thrive. The destruction is part of the process. It cannot be helped or avoided. For us to thrive, destruction is necessary. However, if this is so, why is all this destruction now posing a threat to the planet, a threat to us?

So, what new metaphor can we use to explain and understand things? What new metaphor can give us a knowledge that involves no extracting or deconstituting of anything? What new things can we believe and value that can give rise to this new metaphor? In our current worldview, we believe that we need knowledge to survive and thrive. Knowledge drives progress and makes for prosperity. By any measure, the world will always benefit more from having more love than more knowledge. After all, it was not a lack of knowledge that made for the Holocaust or over 350 years of slavery and segregation in the US. Nor did a lack knowledge make for World War I and II. Neither is a lack of knowledge making for the ecological peril that is now upon us. We therefore need a new metaphor that will always remind us that love is more valuable than knowledge. We also need one that will always remind us that our knowledge is a creature of us, reflecting all we believe and value. Thus, for us to know more, we must be willing to become more. Finally, we need a metaphor that reminds us of how small we are, and thus how little we will ever know. In short, we need a metaphor that will instill humility rather than hubris.

Understandably, mining is a mechanistic metaphor, reflecting the fact that we value machines. We believe that machines are good and necessary. We believe that our prosperity resides in machines, even becoming machines, like cyborgs. Thus, any new metaphor will have to be organic. It will have to put us in harmony with the world's natural rhythms. As of now, I have no command of such a metaphor. However, what I do have are the teachings from all the prophets which say that our redemption resides in how we live rather than how much knowledge we possess.

Fourty Seven

MORAL CONFLICT

Many in philosophy now claim that much of our conflict is moral conflict. What you believe and value conflicts with what I believe and value. When our beliefs and values run deep, compromise is impossible, making conflict inevitable. Violence becomes the only way to resolve the conflict.

But there is another way to navigate moral conflict that avoids violence. Human diversity is like gravity. We can do nothing about it. We will always believe and value different things. Also, no one can change what we believe and value. Further, because our circumstances and experiences will always be different, we will always believe and value different things. However, it is not our diversity that makes for conflict. It is our treating what we believe and value as absolute and complete, and thus beyond criticism. What we believe is perfect because we are supposedly perfect. Consequently, anything that is different to what I represent must is wrong. There would be no racism, dogmatism, militarism, nationalism, tribalism, ethnocentrism, or fundamentalism without narcissism. Narcissism is the beginning of human misery. Even the often intensity and ferocity of human diversity has nothing to do with the making of conflict. Thus, focusing on lessening the intensity and ferocity of human diversity will produce nothing useful. Again, fighting with human diversity is like fighting with gravity. Yet, we continue to believe that needs to be our focus. We need to be always promoting, accommodating, and celebrating diversity. A diversity problem supposedly needs a diversity solution. But again, diversity was never our problem. However, because we believe that diversity is our problem, everything is now upside down. For instance, we now believe that exclusion is wrong. We should value inclusion. However, inclusion has no foundation in the natural world, meaning that no ecology includes all species. Can you put dolphins in all lakes? Grow every plant in the desert? Ecologies discriminate and exclude. Besides being natural, exclusion is necessary. Species and ecologies survive and thrive by cultivating distinction, by obtaining a unique set of abilities. No two ecologies ever possess the same expertise or talents. In this way, exclusion rather than inclusion, is evolutionary. Moreover, excellence fosters exclusion. Excellence means distinguishing ourselves from others through sacrifice, discipline, and perseverance. It is excellence that separates exclusion from inclusion. Inclusion has no ecological foundation because it represents mediocrity, which helps no species survive and thrive. Yet here we are now celebrating inclusion and demonizing exclusion. Another reminder of how we can arrive at a perverse understanding of something.

Ultimately, what moral conflict demands of us is moral consistency. What should be good for the geese, should be good for the gander. In short, moral consistency is about treating both sides evenly and fairly. It demands a moral compass that will allow us to do so. One such compass can be diversity. For the sake of diversity, I must treat both sides evenly and fairly. This means reminding both sides that neither side wants to be victimized and brutalized by the other side. If I allow one side to victimize and brutalize the other side today, then I must allow the other side to do so tomorrow. Thus, for the sake of diversity, maybe we should refrain from victimizing and brutalizing each other. We could also use choice as a moral compass. If I want choice for me, then I should allow choice for thee. So, if I believe I should have the right to control how my life unfolds, including my choices about my body and who

I choose to love, then I should allow you to control how your life unfolds. However, how many of us are morally consistent? It is our hypocrisy that impedes the resolution of moral conflict. In this case, us refusing to submit and conform to the same standards that we are often too eager to impose on others. A lack of moral consistency means a lack of integrity; without integrity, trust and respect become impossible.

So again, moral conflict arises from a lack of moral consistency rather than our diversity. In this way, moral conflict is our making. It reflects a lack of grace and generosity. Moral conflict reminds us why mercy and compassion have ecological foundations. There will always be an occasion when all of us need mercy and compassion.

Fourty Eight

CLIMBING MOUNTAINS

$\mathcal{W}$hy would you want to climb the highest peaks in the world without safety devices? That is, why would you want to consistently demand perfection from yourself? There is no perfection in anything. Nothing about perfection is ecological, meaning life affirming. After perfection, what is possible? What can we learn, where can we grow? Why then should we demand something that is so hostile to life?

We are to be beautifully imperfect — to learn and grow from our mistakes and misfortunes. Thus, to climb the world's highest peaks without safety devices is to defy life's natural order deliberately. We will all make mistakes and encounter misfortune. No amount of skill and preparation will save us from this reality. Safety devices are about humility, recognizing that life will always be much larger than us. There is no way for us to always respond perfectly to everything life sends our way.

Perfectionism is narcissism. This is what makes perfectionism destructive. Perfectionism says that I can become all that I need to become. I can know all that I need to know. I can control everything. Also, perfectionism says that I know all my limits and that I can exceed all my weaknesses. I am in no way susceptible to error, miscalculation, or anything. Consequently, in being perfect, there can be no challenging of my actions and decisions. I am no longer human, as I have no need to learn and grow. Other mortals climb mountains with safety devices. However, because I am perfect, I can do differently. In being a creature of narcissism, perfectionism is no less delusional and destructive than any other creature of narcissism, such as nationalism and fundamentalism. It ultimately makes us closed systems, life negating systems.

But eventually life will disabuse us of our delusions. In being a creature of narcissism, perfectionism makes us ugly. It distorts our sense of nearly everything. For where is our concern for the wellbeing of others when we climb mountains without safety devices? Do we owe our loved ones nothing? Is our life only our life? Where is our obligation to others in our calculation to climb a mountain without safety devices?

Narcissism separates us from others. We assume that our lives are our lives. In this way, narcissism makes us promiscuous by releasing of any kind of relational, communal, or ecological obligation. Conquering this mountain without safety devices is what I need to do to find meaning in life. The reward is purely mine. It will do nothing to make the lives of others better. Yet this is also what makes narcissism so seductive. It saves us from reckoning with each other, and thus owning the fact that we are relational, communal, and ecological beings. If we are ever going to make it out alive, we have to at least care for each other.

Fourty Nine

MULTICULTURALISM

Multiculturalism assumes that we have a diversity problem. Failure to correctly manage our differences will supposedly result in chaos and discord. Thus, for there to be harmony, our differences need to be managed. We supposedly need to develop and implement a vast array of positions and practices that will allow us to do this effectively. Consequently, every organization now has a vast and ever-expanding diversity and inclusion bureaucracy that now include a Chief Diversity Officer, Inclusion Specialists, a Department of Multiculturalism, a Department of Diversity and Inclusion, Rapid Response Bias Teams, a Diversity and Inclusion Council, and an Office of Equal Opportunity, Inclusion, and Resolution Services.

Managing diversity means including and accommodating diversity. Multiculturalism assumes that a diversity problem needs a diversity solution. We fix diversity by attending to diversity. This means hiring and promoting more Black, Brown, and Indigenous peoples. It also means publishing, electing, nominating, honoring, and celebrating more Black, Brown, and Indigenous peoples. It also means guaranteeing that every Black, Brown, and Indigenous person feel valued and included. Never should any such person ever encounter anything that is upsetting, triggering, or traumatizing. All of this perfectly captured in a statement regarding a recent incident:

> Syracuse University unequivocally condemns racism and xenophobia and rejects bigotry, hate and intolerance of any kind. The derogatory language used by a professor on his course syllabus is damaging to the learning environment for our students and offensive to . . . . As a result, a complaint has been filed against the professor with the Office of Equal Opportunity, Inclusion and Resolution Services. The complaint will be investigated and addressed according to procedures set forth in the Faculty Manual. The professor has been placed on administrative leave from teaching and removed from the classroom pending the outcome of a full investigation. . . . We will not allow any member of our community to violate the University's commitment to a safe, inclusive and welcoming learning and living environment.

However, what has emerged from the rise of multiculturalism is a contrived and manufactured diversity, one that has been stripped of all its intensity and ferocity. One that demands investigation, suspension, and termination, rather than communication, mediation, and deliberation. That is, what has emerged is a sterilized and medicalized diversity.

Regardless of our race or creed, human beings need to struggle. Struggle challenges us. Through struggle we become strong and resilient. Through struggle we change and evolve. Through struggle we learn to endure and persevere. In short, through struggle we become better versions of ourselves. To save us from struggle, such as saving us from things that are subjectively believed to be upsetting, is to retard our overall development. Yet, this is what multiculturalism does. Through our vast diversity and inclusion bureaucracy, we have now made it nearly impossible for any Black, Brown, of Indigenous person to encounter anything upsetting. In doing so, we have also impeded Black, Brown, and Indigenous people from acquiring the resources necessary to grow and flourish. On the other hand, because of the harsh consequences that now come with saying or doing anything that could subjectively be seen as upsetting, triggering, or traumatizing, others are less and less willing to be honest and transparent. This, in turn, is making for another set of problems as human beings need to be honest to develop. Being honest and transparent makes us open systems, life affirming systems. In short, being honest and transparent is ecological. Thus, any movement that stops us from being honest and transparent harms us.

Mostly because of multiculturalism, higher education is now fully sterilized, sanitized, and medicalized. In being saved from struggle, we become weak and fragile, laden with all kinds of neuroses and psychoses. We now need more and more safe spaces, trigger warnings, and speech codes. We are now in a full negative feedback loop. As we become increasingly weak and fragile from being saved from struggle, we are becoming more and more neurotic and psychotic, which in turn is making us demand more and more sterilized, sanitized, and medicalized environs and interactions. In turn, such environs and interactions are making us more and more weak and fragile, and thus more and more incapable of struggling, persevering, and overcoming. As a result, we are demanding more and more protections, as in more and more safe spaces, trigger warnings, and speech codes. Ultimately, we are more and more demanding that our organizations do more and more to protect us. Taking care of ourselves, which should be our responsibility, now becomes the responsibility of the organization. Again, this negative feedback loop has now made for the full medicalization of higher education. Multiculturalism has perversely succeeded in infantilizing and pathologizing many of us in higher education. Now learning has become nothing. How can learning occur without confronting potentially upsetting, triggering, and traumatizing things? For learning to occur, the experience must be deeply and profoundly disturbing and disorienting. It must be so because it must challenge us to the core, tormenting everything we believe and value. It should tear us into pieces.

However, multiculturalism makes us silly and stupid by impeding learning and thereby blocking us from growing and evolving. Without the ability to figure out stuff on our own, we have become gullible and desperate. Conse-quently, nothing found in multiculturalism can withstand any kind of rig-orous scrutiny. It is all ignorance and nonsense, hysteria and paranoia. For instance, there is no science that supports trigger warnings. In fact, the science show that trigger warnings harm us. Moreover, the fact that two persons are of the same race means nothing. Such persons can be of fundamentally differ-ent "lived experiences" because of being of different experiences and circum-stances. Human diversity will always exceed the boxes that multiculturalism values. We will always be, in the words of Walt Whitman, multitudes. How-ever, our goal should be to become beautiful multitudes.

Finally, multiculturalism corrupts our understanding of human diversity. Multiculturalism assumes that, if left unmanaged, human diversity can be a problem. It can make for strife and discord. Thus, we supposedly all have a vested interest in managing diversity, which means being ready to make the sacrifices and compromises necessary to manage diversity effectively. For multiculturalism, managing diversity effectively means, among other things, never allowing certain persons to say or do things that will hurt or diminish diversity. But again, behind all of this is the belief that human diversity can threaten us if left unmanaged.

Have human beings ever had a gravity problem? Is there even such a thing as a gravity problem? Indeed, we have never had a gravity problem. We accept the fact that gravity reflects the natural order of things. Just as well, human beings have never had a diversity problem. We will always believe and value different things because of our different experiences and circumstances. History makes no case that our diversity was ever a problem. Like gravity, diversity reflects the natural order of things. Just as we never seek to manage gravity, we should never seek to manage diversity. We should treat diversity like how we treat gravity. Just let it be. It threatens nothing. Instead, what seems like a diversity problem is really one of narcissism — us being convinced that we are perfect in all ways and in all things and thus have the right to impose what we believe and value on others through force and violence. We do this for your sake. It is an act of generosity, another manifestation of how wonderful and perfect we are. However, without narcissism, there would be no racism, militarism, totalitarianism, nationalism, fundamentalism, tribalism, and ethnocentrism. Narcissism is the beginning of human misery. When we become obsessed with ourselves, there is no space or place for others. In other words, narcissism makes communication impossible by making empathy and compassion impossible. However, without communication, all that remains is tension, aggression, and confrontation. This is the threat that narcissism poses. It ultimately promotes distrust and suspicion, discord and animosity, strife and violence.

What then is multiculturalism? It is narcissism or another creature of narcissism. Multiculturalism is us using force and violence to impose our beliefs and values on others. It is us being convinced that our beliefs and values are perfect and superior to all others. Multiculturalism has nothing to do with promoting diversity. It is instead about promoting conformity and homogeneity. In other words, multiculturalism is about erasing, displacing, and destroying human diversity. Instead of diversity, multiculturalism values force and violence. Failure to submit and conform to multiculturalism's values, beliefs, norms, and expectations will result in harsh consequences. The goal is to inflict as much pain as possible. Even the slightest error can result in termination or expulsion.

In having no interest in diversity, multiculturalism has no interest in education or learning. Multiculturalism is about coercion and indoctrination. We will do everything possible to impose our beliefs and values on you. You will have no choice in the end. Submit or suffer the consequences. In this way, multiculturalism reinforces the belief that violence is good and necessary. In this case, violence is supposedly integral to successfully managing diversity. It serves a higher cause. For multiculturalism, saving us from violence is like sparing the child the rod. Yes, violence will bring misery, but it is supposedly necessary. Thus, what cannot be missed about multiculturalism is the totalitarianism, the determination to ban, cancel, and deplatform any person who represents values and beliefs different to our own. There will be no diversity in our diversity.

For multiculturalism, diversity means conformity, valuing and believing what we believe and value. Thus, with multiculturalism, there is no democracy or willingness to make space and time for truths and views different from our own. We are to assume that the world is inherently monologic, it lends for only one set of truths. Multiculturalism, of course, supposedly represents this set of truths. We merely have to look at the surveys to see what multiculturalism is doing to us. Most college students now say that they are afraid to be honest and transparent in the classroom for fear of being punished for saying something a person may view as offensive. Another majority of college students say they will report any fellow student who says something offensive in a class. This is what totalitarianism looks like, being completely convinced that what you are doing is right and just, and thus beyond error and criticism. In this case, in protecting others from being hurt, you are making the world. You are oblivious to your narcissism. You have no awareness of how destructive your righteousness is, impeding your growth and development. But again, in saving you from diversity, multiculturalism is saving from learning, beginning with learning who and what you are and how you became what and who you are. So now, anything you find upsetting or disturbing, you can simply name as xenophobic, homophobic, or misogynistic, and you are released from struggling with it. In saving you from diversity, in saving you from learning, multiculturalism has made the world safe for you, or has made for the impression that it is doing so. This is how multiculturalism seduces us, by promising safety. No different to the safety that our increasingly neurotic and psychotic parents are also seeking to give us. However, nothing in psychology supports this kind of safety. Safety stunts our development. It stops us from venturing out and testing our limits. Moreover, safety distorts our understanding of life. Life is all about risks. We often have no clue where these risks will arise. However, we have to acquire the ability to navigate and manage these risks. This is on us. To depend on others to do this for is to become codependent, and this never ends well. Indeed, being able to navigate and manage risks is a reliable measure of mental health. But again, multiculturalism seduces us through the promise of safety. Its vast and ever-expanding bureaucracy will protect us from any person or thing that threatens to harm or diminish us. This includes words, books, films, songs, objects, costumes, and even rocks. Never again will we be triggered or traumatized.

In many ways, multiculturalism represents our narrative of progress. We supposedly achieve progress by either neutralizing or smashing human diversity. Conformity is good, conformity is necessary. We supposedly achieve progress through the rise of institutions that will bring order and control. Institutions will successfully do this by imposing a vision on us, using rules and regulations, practices and structures, to do so. This is the work of multiculturalism — using the pretext of diversity to promote conformity. Yet, the reality is that no institution can genuinely promote diversity and remain an institution. Diversity upends hierarchy. Diversity means liberty, being able to believe and value different things, and thus being able to live and behave differently. Diversity undermines the conformity that makes institutions possible. But now the world is different. No longer can institutions depend on segregation and immigration laws to suppress human diversity. Now diversity must be neutralized and suppressed by other means. We must coopt it. This is the work of multiculturalism, and it is doing it, by any measure, exceptionally well.

Progress means that multiculturalism is the most effective weapon against human diversity and all it represents and promises. It has perversely succeeded in weaponizing diversity against diversity. In the end, this is the most serious threat that multiculturalism poses to us. Our redemption is bound up with our diversity. The more successful we become in destroying and vanquishing our diversity, the more perilous our lives become. Multiculturalism puts us on the wrong side of history. We survive and thrive by becoming more and more diverse. Diversity is what the world demands of us. It is why so much of the world is dark matter and dark energy. It is why words will never lend for one meaning. It is why meaning and ambiguity are bound up with each other. That there is no diversity without liberty means that, in the end, multiculturalism robs us of our beauty and humanity.

Fifty

Dark Matter, Dark Energy

Most of the universe is dark matter and dark energy. However, when we read about dark matter and dark energy, we tend to come away with the impression that we are speaking about a world that is outside and separate from us. That is, we are objectively describing something that is out there in the world. However, dark matter and dark energy are all around us. More than the universe, life is mostly dark matter and dark energy. Who, after all, knows what life will send our way tomorrow, or next week?

How much do we really know about ourselves? Analysts now tell us that claiming to know our own minds is folly. What then is the moral of the story regarding dark matter and dark energy? It means that our knowledge of anything will always be insignificant. We will never have the means to meaningfully unpack the mystery of life. Thus, our lives cannot be about acquiring and generating knowledge on the premise that we can fulfill this mission, demystify life. It must be about something else. It must be about how we live and treat each other. For note Christ's commandment calling us to love each other. Note also that Muhammad could neither read nor write.

Science assumes that we can command life's mystery. But dark matter and dark energy tell us differently. History also tells us differently, meaning that none of our horrors we can blame on a lack of knowledge. Dark matter and dark energy reveal that life is generative. We should be about embracing the unknown, rather than trying to conquer it. This would mean recognizing that ignorance can often be liberating and affirming. Rather than an absence of knowledge, ignorance can be awe. It can also be humility and faith, patience and tolerance. After all, an absence of knowledge is merely that, an absence of knowledge. It does not mean that there is an absence of awe, an absence of love, an absence of mercy, an absence of compassion. Neither does it mean that there is an absence of kindness and tenderness. So again, why must we be obsessed with knowledge? How did we ever come to believe that our prosperity resides in acquiring more and more knowledge?

We merely must look at what is happening worldwide to recognize that colonization can be insidious. Now nearly all the peoples around the world are obsessed with acquiring more and more knowledge, and training and schooling more and more people to secure this knowledge. We now all believe that our prosperity resides in knowledge. Such is the nature of neocolonialism; we now all believe and value the same things.

Dark matter and dark energy remind us that we will never know much about God. Yet this ignorance in no way impedes or lessens any relationship we can have with God. In fact, a God of boundless mystery is far more valuable to us than one that is less so. For sure, such a God will never make us dogmatic and autocratic, and, in so doing, put us at each other's throats. Instead, embracing a God of boundless mystery will make us dialogic, pluralistic, and democratic, always reminding us of how small we are. In making us so, such a God will make us beautiful, and in becoming so we will make the world and each other so. Thus, rather than becoming knowledgeable, our redemption resides in becoming beautiful.

Fifty One

PERSUASION

On second thought, maybe the Greeks are correct — communication is about persuasion. After all, what is slavery, us persuading others that one group has the right to brutalize another group. What is the Holocaust, one group persuading another group that it has the right to exterminate another group. What is capitalism, being persuaded that competition is the natural order of things. What is liberalism, socialism, and conservatism? We must even be persuaded that communication is about persuasion. Suffice it to say, persuasion is all around us. All our institutions are based on persuasion. We are always persuading others as to why our institutions are important. When we can no longer effectively do so, our institutions implode and collapse. This is another way to look at politics, different sides trying to persuade us in different ways that often make for tension and conflict.

Because Greek civilization was based on subjugation, discrimination, and oppression, the Greeks had a lot of explaining to do. For instance, for the enslaved in Greek society, nothing about slavery is obvious. That our own civilization is based on Greek civilization, with all the same subjugation, discrimination, and oppression, also mean that we have a lot of explaining to do. We can therefore now understand why viewing communication as persuasion makes sense for us and the Greeks. Almost nothing of what we believe and value is obvious to all. We therefore have to persuade ourselves and each other that the things we believe and value are true. The most effective form of persuasion is when we can make others believe that we are merely describing when in fact we are persuading. That is, the most effective kind of persuasion is when we can mask the fact that what we are doing has nothing to do with ideology, power, and politics. Persuasion is thus most effective when it is invisible.

But should persuasion govern our affairs? Does persuasion make the world better? In what ways is persuasion helpful and valuable? Would there have been slavery, Jim Crow, and the Holocaust without persuasion? Persuasion is narcissism. It says that I want you to look at the world the way I do because it serves my needs and interests. Thus, persuasion assumes that there is nothing wrong if I succeed in having you believe and value what I believe and value. There is therefore nothing wrong about I trying to make the world less diverse. Persuasion is all politics, meaning that persuasion has no interest in whether what I believe is right or wrong, constructive or destructive. All that matters is whether I can make you view things the way I do. The measure of persuasion is agreement. The goal of persuasion is to end disagreement. Persuasion is always devising new ways to accomplish this goal. But one major fallout from persuasion is us being distrustful of disagreement. We associate disagreement with chaos and disunity. We have neither patience nor tolerance for disagreement. For us, disagreement represents a negative force that we must neutralize. It supposedly threatens our prosperity. Something must be done about it. It cannot stand. Indeed, herein resides the origins of persuasion, convincing ourselves and each other that disagreement is bad. However, there is nothing bad about disagreement. Disagreement merely means that I view something different to the way you do. It assumes there is never any one right or perfect way to look at anything. Disagreement means diversity. We are hostile to disagreement because it challenges our narcissism, us believing that our view of things is always right and perfect. So, a world without persuasion would be one without narcissism, and a world without narcissism would be one without militarism, tribalism, nationalism, fundamentalism, racism, and other progeny of narcissism. In short, a world without persuasion would be a much better one. There would be for certain a lot of disagreement and diversity, but no misery and destruction.

Let us then begin to work towards achieving this world devoid of persuasion. We do so by ending our own need to persuade, coerce, and subdue. This means working on identifying and ending our own egotism and narcissism. We can do this by doing much less talking and much more listening, observing, and reflecting. We can also do this by always attending to our assumptions, ultimately seeking to empty our minds of them. In Buddhism this is called the empty mind. Only an empty mind is an open mind. We can also achieve a world without persuasion by always reminding ourselves of our insignificance. From the perspective of the universe, we are nothing. Finally, we can achieve a world without persuasion by never allowing our desires and passions to rule us, meaning never allowing the body to control the mind. This is one of the most important teachings found in Hinduism — never allowing our senses to rule us.

Persuasion is of a worldview that values force and violence. Moving beyond persuasion will therefore demand releasing ourselves of this worldview.

Fifty Two

FREE SPEECH

The notion is free speech is just as absurd and dangerous as the notion of hate speech. For when is speech ever free, as in being released of consequences and implications? How many times do we pay no social, financial, or professional price for saying something others dislike? Moreover, the notion of free speech means that all speech is free. We supposedly both get the say what we want. However, because our resources are different, our megaphones are different. In fact, some of us may have no megaphones are all. Who your speech can reach can be different to who my speech can reach. Consequently, even though my speech can technically be better for a community than yours, your speech be much more influential. Further, free speech can mean false speech. What then is the value of free speech when it is false? In fact, free speech puts no organic pressure on us to be honest and transparent. Free speech is meant to serve the individual. It assumes that we are persons rather than relationships. Supposedly, what matters, first and foremost, is my right to say whatever I want to say. How what I say impacts you is secondary. Again, in most cases, free speech has no concern with whether what I say is true or false. Free speech is all about freedom. We believe that freedom is about rights that belong to the individual. Free speech is about the right of the individual to speak freely. When an individual can do so, this supposedly makes for a robust and vibrant society. We get introduced to all kinds of ideas. Free speech supposedly reflects a democratic and pluralistic society. In fact, for many, free speech is the cornerstone of such a society. However, many are now asking what becomes of that society when much of the free speech is deliberately false? This is no doubt a fair concern. But I have a different concern. What makes us human, simply speaking freely or speaking genuinely and compassionately? Why, then, our insistence on the low standard? Why our unwillingness to insist that we speak genuinely and compassionately rather than merely freely? What stops us from making this demand, especially when speaking genuinely and compassionately does not lessen our ability to speak freely.

The notion of free speech is yet to come to terms with the fact that we are relational and ecological beings. Speech always has consequences. For our ecologies to thrive, our speech must serve a larger good. It must serve the best interests of others. The reason being, that in any relationship or ecology, our own prosperity is bound up with the prosperity of others. For us to thrive, others must thrive. Thus, our speech cannot merely be about advancing what is best for us. It must be about advancing what is best for all of us.

What is therefore most dangerous about the notion of free speech is that it deepens our narcissism. It is all about indulging the desires and passions of the individual. So again, free speech is often about the right to express what I feel. Whether what I feel is true or false is secondary. Whether what I feel is valuable to others is also secondary. All that matters is my right to express what I feel. However, such a right has no relational or ecological foundation. Nothing about it is therefore life affirming. This is the final indictment against the notion of free speech. It is born of a civilization that devalues life in all its possibilities and fecundities.

Fifty Three

HUMILITY

*L*ove, compassion, mercy, would all be great. But what we need most is humility — recognizing that we know almost nothing and will never know much more. For instance, who made God? What was the bang that set off the Big Bang? Do we know how we will look at things in five years, ten years, twenty years? Do we know what things will change our life? Do we know the people who will change our life? Do we know what happens after death? Yet in the face of so much unknown, so much dark matter and dark energy, we remain arrogant and belligerent. We continue to believe that we can know things completely and perfectly. There is no need for humility.

We are therefore always assuming that we know exactly what a person intends or means. This is the first problem. Without humility, communication perishes. For if you already know what I intend or mean, what becomes the purpose of communication? The next problem concerns gratitude, being able to recognize what we are fortunate to have. In reality, life owes us nothing. Life is about perspective. Humility makes gratitude possible. The humbler we become, the larger our perspective. Humility stops us from envying and yearning for what others possess. Finally, humility saves us from the ravages of certainty. Certainty means not only I am right, but I am completely and absolutely right. I am devoid of doubt. So once again there is no reason for communication. If what you have is different to what I have, then you are wrong. Nothing further needs to be discussed. No doubt, certainty is seductive. It saves us from doing a lot of hard work, like sustaining doubt or challenging all that we believe and value. In this way, certainty makes us lazy. It stops us from probing and questioning. It also stops us from compromising because compromise requires flexibility and elasticity. However, without being able to compromise, progress in a multicultural world becomes all but impossible. Yet, there is no rigidity in the natural world. Open systems, meaning living systems, promote hybridity and permeability. Such systems evolve and change through exchange and intercourse. Rigidity means death. Thus, from an ecological perspective, certainty is an abomination. It stops us from growing and evolving.

We need look no further than history to make this point about certainty. When we find human misery, we always find an absence of humility. By impeding communication, certainty makes violence inevitable. By impeding compromise, certainty makes violence inevitable. This is arguably why God wants nothing to do with certainty. Certainty is for fanatics, those who murder and oppress. God wants us to be of faith. Faith means humility. I will never know God completely and perfectly. God is too profound to conform to my imagination. Thus, my mind and heart will always remain open. I will never foster the impression that my understanding of God is final. Instead, my spiritual practice will be about instilling humility and cultivating gratitude. In being of such a practice, I will choose peace over violence, dialogue over monologue, and diversity over conformity. Humility is much more than changing how we view things. It is about changing how we embody things. That God demands humility from us reminds us that God wants us to be beautiful. Only in becoming beautiful we make the world and each other so.

Fifty Four

INFORMATION

There was once a time when God was preeminent. We looked to God to know everything. There was also once a time when nature was preeminent. Now information is preeminent. We believe that we can now generate all the information we need to live a good and meaningful life. Never again will we ever have to look to anything else for solutions and answers. Information is the new end of history. We are advised to do nothing, absolutely nothing, to impede the ascendance of information.

We assume that our problems arise from a lack of information. In solving our problems, information will make our lives better. However, let us keep in mind that our problems, or those that make for the most misery and destruction, never had anything to do with a lack of information. Slavery had nothing to do with a lack of information. So also, the Holocaust. So also, apartheid. So also, Jim Crow. So also, World I and II. There is simply no correlation between information and the end of human misery. But the age of information is now upon us. Now we frame everything as an information problem. An information problem needs an information solution. This is what neocolonialism looks like in the twenty-first century. Regardless of race or creed, we supposedly all have information problems that need information solutions.

We therefore all now need the expertise and machines that will allow us to acquire all the information we now need to achieve the prosperity that information promises.

There is a lot about information that is seductive. Information says that our problems are not of our making. They are problems of information, or lack thereof. In finally being able to generate all the information we need, we will fix these problems. Moreover, information assumes that our problems are fixable. With enough information, we can fix almost every problem. In this way, information supposedly gives us control over our destiny.

Information is alienation. It is us separating ourselves from ourselves. This is also what makes information so seductive. If our problems supposedly have nothing to do with us, then the solution to them supposedly have nothing to do with us. Thus, rather than challenging us to own our involvement in making our problems, information releases us from doing so. Nothing about how we live or what we believe and value deserves examination or correction. Even when the problem is us, information promises to fix it for us. No heavy lifting will we ever have to do. Indeed, the goal of information is to save us from struggle. However, in saving us from struggle, information impedes our development. This is also how information sets off a negative feedback loop. As we become more and more alienated, we become more and more amenable to information, which in turn makes us more and more alienated. Thus, what cannot be missed with the rise of information is the rise of social isolation and the misery this condition creates. We are now in a full mental health crisis. Social isolation is at the center of it, and technology is driving it. Never before have we been exposed to so much information. Social isolation is us becoming closed systems, dying systems. It is un turning inward, never learning to confront demanding and threatening things. So with the rise of social isolation comes the rise of safe spaces and trigger warnings. We must be protected from almost everything that could be upsetting. Such again is the negative feedback loop that is now upon us — alienation, social isolation, and information driving and reproducing each other.

The impression we now have is that information will end well for us. Information will give us a near perfect world. Information will make our roads safer. Information will end diseases. Information will make our offspring healthy. Information will give us better medicines. Information will make for less deviancy and criminality. Information will make the growing of food more efficient and abundant. Information will give us more compatible life partners. Information will make for a better match between employees and employers. Information will enhance learning. Information will make for cheaper goods by making manufacturing more efficient. For doing all these wonderful things, we are to thank not merely information, but all the machines that are generating and providing us with all this information. However, this will always be a world of laws and limits. No amount of information will ever allow us to defy these laws and limits without facing the consequences for doing so. Information is born of our alienation, and our deepening alienation is driving the rise of information. As we become more and more separated from ourselves, we are also becoming more and more separated from the world and each other. What this means is that nearly all the information we are now obsessively generating is good for nothing. This information is coming from a place of alienation, a place of death. In fact, more than useless, this information is destructive.

Fifty Five

ANIMAL RIGHTS

The question we are now asking is whether animals should have rights like ours. That we are now seriously asking this question is seen as a sign of moral and cultural progress. But this is the wrong question. A better question is why should we have the rights we now have, such as the right to eat other animals, to cage and capture other animals, to live in ways that make for the eradication of other animals, to destroy other animals' habitats, to poison all the rivers, streams, and oceans, and to even destroy the planet? Why must we continue to have all these rights? What is our defense? How do we legally defend our moral authority to be the arbitrators of who gets rights, especially when no dog, dolphin, or whale has plans to do to us what we do to them?

We contend that culture gives us this authority. Because we have culture, we are superior to animals. Supposedly, after acquiring a superior linguistic and symbolic capacity, because of evolutionary pressures, culture came next. Then culture made for science and technology. Thus, for us, culture is the point of separation and distinction. We can never have too much culture. However, where in history can we make the case that culture has made us morally superior to animals? Have dogs ever enslaved other dogs? Do dolphins do mass incarceration? Do elephants pollute and contaminate all the world's rivers, streams, and oceans? Do rabbits have a Holocaust? Do goats now threaten to destroy the planet with weapons of mass destruction? Do cats have a World War I and II? What then is to be made with our obsession with culture? Maybe it is time for us to begin viewing ourselves in ecological terms rather than cultural terms. We can begin to do so by ridding language of culture. Maybe we have too much culture.

Our relationship to language should be natural. We should just be able to open our mouths and speak. But because of culture, language is now unnatural. We have added all kinds of arbitrary rules to language to make it orderly and uniform. We believe that without all these rules, such as allowing for goose and geese, but no moose and "meese," language will descend into chaos, ultimately making communication impossible. But linguists have long known that these rules are arbitrary, silly, and unnecessary. They corrupt our natural relationship to language. All languages are inherently orderly and equally capable of expressing complex thought. The distinction between a language and a dialect is purely of our making. It has no basis in the nature of language. It is about power. Those who have power are described as having a language, and those without are described as having a dialect. However, the rules we have imposed on language are much more than silly, arbitrary, and unnecessary. They are destructive, harming the relationship between language and mind. We do much more than speak a language. We embody a language. Thus, any disruption of language disrupts us to the core. Just as much as we make ourselves in language, language makes us. In short, language makes minds and minds make language. Consequently, there is no separation between mind, society and language. All make each other. To limit how we live in language is to limit how we relate to ourselves and each other. In this case, liberation is about releasing our minds of all the rules that culture has imposed on us through language.

We could also rid ourselves of culture by undermining hierarchy. We hear again and again that hierarchy is natural and necessary. Hierarchy reflects inequality, supposedly. Just like how certain species are supposedly superior to other species, certain humans are also superior to others. However, advocates of hierarchy tend to be oblivious to the fact that any definition of superiority is, first and foremost, cultural rather than natural. What we judge and perceive to be so reflects our beliefs and values. In fact, biologists now tell us that the most reliable measure of the health and vitality of any ecology can be found in looking at the most vulnerable species in it. Regardless of how strong and magnificent any species is, no species can survive and thrive in a dying ecology. So, whereas advocates of hierarchy encourage us to focus on the strongest species, we should really be focusing on the weak. Further, advocates of hierarchy claim that hierarchy represents the fact that competition is the order of things. Supposedly, life only rewards the fittest, strongest, and brightest. We hear again and again that competition saves us from mediocrity. It allows the best to rise to the top.

However, analysts now tell us that evolution eventually turns competition into cooperation. Competition impedes evolution by fostering fear, distrust, and suspicion. Cooperation becomes a better strategy for surviving and thriving. Finally, all the rules and regulations, procedures and arrangements, which make for hierarchy harm us by institutionalizing us, that is, by making us dependent and co-dependent. Hierarchy stops us from finding our way in the world. We can only do so through struggle, by facing life honestly and courageously. Through struggle we become strong, resilient, and independent. Thus, by institutionalizing us, hierarchy impedes our flourishing. It stops us from doing all the hard and difficult work we need to do to survive and thrive.

Culture is us making believe that we are superior to animals. But what is so wrong about being an animal or embracing our animality? How many things do animals do that are more life negating than what we do with all our culture? Again, maybe we are asking the wrong question. Rather than focusing on how we can fix our culture and make it better for everyone, maybe we should be focusing on how to lessen our obsession with culture. What would the world look like if we began on the premise that we are first and foremost ecological beings rather than cultural beings? It will, by any measure, certainly be a much less destructive world.

Epilogue

What is the purpose of learning? What does learning demand of us? What does it mean to be learned? What does it promise? I have long been grappling with these questions. I once believed that the purpose of learning was to enlarge how we perceive, experience and make sense of things. Another time I believed that the purpose of learning was to free us from fear. To an extent, I still believe these things. But now I believe that the purpose of learning is to cultivate our capacity to love. Love is the negation of all that threatens us, such as hate, malice, and prejudice.

Evidently, I never believed that learning had much to do with knowledge. We can be knowledgeable and still be morally depraved. The reason being that acquiring knowledge can happen without other things happening. We can become knowledgeable by simply consuming vast quantities of information. We can therefore acquire vast bodies of information without changing what we believe and value. In this case, knowledge becomes empty calories. Learning, on the other hand, is about expanding our minds by expanding our hearts. Learning assumes that affairs of the mind are affairs of the heart. To see more we must be willing to believe more. Learning assumes that there can be no opening of the mind without opening the heart. The challenge of learning is finding ways to open our hearts. That is, how do we encourage others to care more about the world, each other, and even ourselves?

Why learning? Learning transforms us by enlarging us. Ultimately, the purpose of learning is to redeem us, to save us from worse instincts and impulses. As we care more, believe more, empathize more, forgive more, share more, love more, we become capable of understanding, experiencing, and becoming much more. In this way, learning makes us stronger, more capable of controlling our worse instincts and impulses. More importantly, by encouraging us to care more, believe more, empathize more, forgive more, share more, and love more, learning makes us beautiful. Thus, the ultimate purpose of learning is to make us beautiful. For only in becoming beautiful we make our worlds and each other so. So, this should be the measure of learning — is what you are reading and studying making you beautiful? Is the exercise or assignment encouraging you to care more, believe more, empathize more, forgive more, share more, love more?

There is an important distinction between learning and schooling. Schooling is about equipping us with expertise and knowledge. The goal is to find the most efficient and effective means to do so. Schooling assumes that learning can be measured. We can have learning outcomes that are quantifiable and measurable. However, what to make now of all our investment in schooling? Did schooling save us from over 350 years of slavery and Jim Crow? Did it save us from the Holocaust? Is it saving us from the creation and proliferation of weapons of mass destruction? Is it saving us from mass incarceration? Is it saving us from destroying the planet? What then is the value of all our schooling? Where is the evidence that those who have more schooling are morally superior to those who have less? Why then must we persist in this schooling enterprise? We could even argue, as others have already done, that schooling does more harm than good by institutionalizing us. But we will leave that discussion for another time.

This book came from a place of learning. It is about I trying to care more, empathize more, love more. I hope in some way it deepens your learning. For in the end, this is the best we can do, help each other become more beautiful.

References

Deetz, S. (1992). *Democracy in an age of corporate colonization: Developments in communication and the politics of everyday life.* New York: SUNY Press.

Satchidananda, Sri Swami (Translation and Commentary) (2020). *The Yoga Sutras of Patanjali.* Yogaville, VA: Integral Yoga Publications.

About the Author

Amardo Rodriguez (Ph.D., Howard University) is a Professor in the Communication and Rhetorical Studies Department at Syracuse University, Syracuse, New York. His research interest is in postcolonial theory, specifically in postcolonizing communication studies. His most recent book-length monograph, *Against DEI: On the End of Language and Difference,* was published by Public Square Press. He has also published papers in such journals as, *Journal of Race & Policy, Journal of Latino/Latin American Studies, Cultural Studies/Critical Methodologies*, and *International Journal of Discrimination and the Law.* Prof. Rodriguez teaches in areas related to communication theory and inquiry. Classes include *Dialogue and Experience, Foundations of Communication Inquiry, Introduction to Communication Theory*, and *Cosmopolitanism & Communication.* He is the Book Review Editor for the *Journal of Race & Policy*